"Could this be Father Bellini's?" Steinberg was holding a Roman collar streaked with blood.

McConnell took it and examined the way the button in the back appeared to have been ripped out. "Good grief, Lieutenant, do you think Joseph has come to harm?"

"We don't know, Monsignor. That's why we're here."

"You say you found Father Bellini's car at the old Lutz place?" McConnell asked.

Steinberg nodded. "Yes, sir. Are you familiar with it?"

McConnell sagged wearily back in his chair with his eyes closed. "Oh, God," he moaned, "not again."

AMITYVILLE
The Nightmare Continues

ROBIN KARL

LEISURE BOOKS   NEW YORK CITY

Dedicated John Myron Kelly.
You were right—there is something besides logic.
Special thanks to:
Rev. Paul Howerton
Father Clem Dorsey
and
Dr. Arnold Spencer Freeman

A LEISURE BOOK ®

July 1991

Published by

Dorchester Publishing Co., Inc.
276 Fifth Avenue
New York, NY 10001

Printed in the United States of America.

... AN AUTHOR'S NOTE ...

For whatever reason, I did not get around to reading Jay Anson's phenomenal best seller, *The Amityville Horror*, until long after it had disappeared from the best seller lists. I read it then only because a friend recommended it. "You'll love it," John said. He was right; I did.

That friend was John Myron Kelly, lawyer by vocation, parapsychologist by avocation, and a man with an avid interest in what can only be termed the bizarre and unusual.

My guess would be that most of the people who read Anson's book mused briefly after completing it, a few debated its authenticity for a like period of time, but all went on to other things. Note: I say "most of the people." John Myron Kelly does not fit that profile.

At the time, when John was living in New York, he became enthralled with the events that occurred at 112 Ocean Avenue. Kristen Kelly, John's wife, would later confide that she was worried about her husband. At one point she was even convinced that he was having an affair. John, it seems, spent an inordinate amount of time "out on the island," rummaging around the focal point of Anson's book.

Three years ago, by juggling schedules, John and I managed to attend the same conference. He used that occasion to hand me a battered diary that he had purchased, along with a number of other books, at a garage sale in Amityville.

"Read it," he said, "then call me."

It was several days, perhaps weeks, before I got around to reading the voluminous tome. It was indeed a diary, and it was also one of the most comprehensive and extensive excursions into the chaotic world of nightmares and terrifying events that I have ever read. It was written at times in an often exquisite style with what are the painfully learned lessons in penmanship that determined and well-intentioned nuns dutifully hammer into the malleable brains of their young charges. At other times, the entries were barely legible and clearly demonstrated the unfathomable anguish the writer was experiencing.

I was fascinated by what appeared to be the writer's near fanatical commitment to record the events that occurred during this period.

Other parts of the journal were not nearly so comprehensive.

When I called John to tell him that I had finished reading the journal, he informed me that he had spent much of his leisure time during the previous year and a half researching the incidents the writer had so carefully recorded. In addition, he had accumulated a comprehensive file that included the journal, copies of records, newspaper accounts, and hours of taped interviews with several of the people either directly or peripherally involved with these events.

I asked the obvious question: "What for?"

"I want you to turn this into a book," he told me.

I do not remember the exact sequence, but there was laughter, periods of uncomfortable silence, throat clearings and comments about being too busy—all mine.

John was undaunted. "Think about it," he said.

We exchanged a few more pleasantries during which time I reluctantly agreed to "think about it," and we hung up.

Three days later, John's complete file arrived by parcel post. The package stayed in the corner of my cluttered office for nearly a month before I relented. The contents should not have surprised me. John has always been the paragon of organization. All of the materials were cataloged. There were maps, a detailed calendar with time notations, a few snapshots, and an 8 x 10 photograph of a forlorn multistoried house. It was boarded up, sadly in need of repair and suffering from either neglect or avoidance or both.

I called John on a Sunday. "Hell, John, you don't need me to write this book; you've got it all organized. Just sit down and write it. The hard parts behind you."

"When are you coming to New York?" he interrupted.

"Too busy. I've got projects laid out for the next eighteen months."

John Kelly, however, was a man on a mission. A short time later, I relented and agreed to meet him in New York for the sole purpose of discussing the book.

I arrived in New York on a Sunday morning, August 13th, and called John's house when he did not meet me at the appointed time and place in the TWA terminal. It was a quirk in John's makeup—he was never on time. Kristen's younger sister, Megan, answered the phone.

She informed me that John was dead; killed in a grinding head-on crash on the Southern State Parkway the previous evening. John had been to Amityville to arrange an interview schedule for me.

I stayed for the funeral, sat through the Requiem Mass and did what I could to console the family. In the end, there was very little I could do. On Thursday, following the funeral, I returned home.

I did not begin the project for two years.

What you are about to read is the book John Kelly wanted to write. In it, you will find events best described as curious, sometimes intriguing —and frequently disturbing.

I hope that John feels, wherever he is, that I have done his project justice.

Reconstructing something interesting and readable from someone else's notes, no matter how well-organized, requires a certain amount of creative license. I have taken that license only when necessary, but I have taken it. The words are mine—the facts were collected by John.

There is, in an effort of this nature, what can be termed an "inclusion quandary." In other words, there was no one perfect place to use the information because it happened outside the flow of chronological events or became apparent as the book was constructed. To address that problem, I used AUTHOR'S NOTES. I sincerely hope that the reader does not find this unscholarly practice to be too disruptive.

Lastly, the names and some identifying details of certain individuals and places mentioned in this book have been changed to protect the great American penchant for privacy.

. . . BACKGROUND . . .

On December 18, 1975, George and Kathy Lutz moved into a house at 112 Ocean Avenue in Amityville, New York. That house was witness to a mass murder in which six people were killed. Subsequent investigation showed that the multistory building, constructed along the banks of the Amityville River, was situated on or close to an area where Shinnecock Indians isolated tribal members judged to be sick or mad. It was also said to be the area where John Ketcham, a practioner of witchcraft, was buried.

During their 28-day tenure in that house, the Lutzes were subjected to a terrifying series of bizarre events that included unexplained footprints in the snow, doors ripped off hinges, windows opening and closing of their own volition, periods of levitation, a ceramic lion that moved about the house, unseen marching bands, moving furniture, strange voices, secret rooms that gave off the odor of human excrement, ghostly visions, bodily harm, unexplained fluctuating temperatures within the house, periods of near-psychotic depression and numerous other misfortunes. Even the priest who blessed their house was drawn into this sinister and mind-numbing series of horrifying events.

On January 14, 1976, the Lutz family fled the house at 112 Ocean Avenue. Unfortunately for the rest of the residents of Amityville, the house remained.

. . . DAY ONE . . .

Donald "Kooch" Webster and Lester Allen Chambers, both eleven, were riding in the parish school bus. It was Wednesday, October 13th. The boys were on their way home from Saint Alomar Academy in Glencoe, Long Island. Sixth graders, they recently had become acquainted.

Kooch, up until the current academic year, had been a student at Brooklyn's Precious Blood School for Boys. He had moved to Amityville during the summer recess.

Kooch Webster lived at 1414 Summer Park Boulevard with his recently divorced mother, Charla. Lester resided at 3257 Oak Street with his sister, Ellen, his father, Roy, and his new stepmother, Alice, a woman he knew almost nothing about aside from the fact that she was a nun prior to marrying his father.

Kooch, seven months younger than his counterpart, was distinguishable from Lester for a variety of reasons. He was small for his age, precocious by nature, bright and energetic. The records that accompanied his transfer from Precious Blood, for whatever reason, did not reveal that he was a student with discipline problems. On two separate occasions during the previous school year, Kooch was reprimanded for possessing marijuana. The first time, he was caught smoking in the boy's rest room, and on the second occasion, the substance was discovered in his locker. In keeping with school policy, his mother was informed of the first infraction, and he was expelled for three days for his second offense. That same school policy dictated that school officials refrain from notifying the police.

Lester, on the other hand, was overweight, "slow" by test standards and tended to exhibit little interest in academics. His father, Roy Chambers, had been repeatedly apprised of his son's below average performance in the classroom. To Lester's credit, however, was the fact that he was known to his teachers at Saint Alomar as polite, thoughtful and conscientious.

As the school bus entered the village of Amityville, it turned left off of Meyer Road and headed east on Ocean Boulevard. The bus's regular route took them past 112 Ocean Avenue, unquestionably one of the most celebrated addresses in the tiny village of approximately 10,000 inhabitants.

When the bus passed 112 Ocean Avenue, the boys turned their conversation, as they had every day for the past week, to the long-abandoned former Lutz house.

"Damn," Kooch whispered, "that old dump sure looks spooky. I'll bet anything that's the place my dad was tellin' me about when he found out me and mom was movin' to Amityville."

Lester shrugged because it was easier than answering—and because his mouth was full. Students at Saint Alomar were forbidden to chew gum in the classroom, and his after-school ritual consisted of stuffing all five sticks of a pack of Juicy Fruit in his mouth as he boarded the bus. The feat accomplished two things; it satisfied his craving for food, understandable to Lester's way of thinking because by that time he had gone for three whole hours without anything to eat, and it served to remind him that he wasn't supposed to talk on the bus. Mrs. Camino, the driver, was the strictest of all the drivers at Saint Almomar; she did not want the kids to talk because she felt that their voices distracted her when she was driving.

Lester was attracted to Kooch Webster because Kooch was what Lester called the adventuresome type. To Lester's way of thinking, Kooch wasn't afraid to try anything. Kooch made a game of not getting caught. Even now he was sliding down in the seat so Mrs. Camino couldn't see him in her oversized rearview mirror. Then, as if driven to really tempt the gods, Kooch took out one of the "sticks" he had purchased from Moe, the pusher down on Capitol Street, and lit up. He cupped his hand over his mouth and exhaled through the thin opening between the bus window and the casing. Despite his precautions, a pencil-thin spiral of smoke still managed to stay in the bus and hover over their heads. Lester was convinced that if Mrs. Camino wasn't already wise to Kooch's little trick, it was only a matter of time until she would be. His only real concern was that the woman might think he was smoking, too. But Lester knew that even if Kooch did get caught, things would still turn out all right because Lester believed Kooch Webster was clever enough to talk his way out of almost anything. On the other hand, Lester also knew that if his father got a report that he was smoking, there would be hell to pay.

"My dad told me about some guy that killed his whole family in a house here in Amityville," Kooch continued to whisper. "He even showed me the stuff he cut out of the papers and put in his scrapbook."

"Your old man saves newspaper clippings of murders?"

"Yeah, you should see it. He's got all kinds of weird shit in that scrapbook of his. He knows all about killers like Manson and Oswald and some guy named Ruby."

"Aw, Ruby ain't a guy's name. It's a girl's

name." There were some things that Lester was sure of, and Ruby being a girl's name was one of them.

Kooch's face deteriorated into an impatient scowl. Every now and then it was apparent, even to Kooch, why Lester had to spend so much time in Saint Alomar's remedial classes. To entertain himself as much as bestow knowledge on his dimwitted friend, Kooch proceeded to launch into a long and unnecessarily gory description of what happened that fateful day in Dallas.

Lester listened as Kooch, voice muffled, gave a detailed account interrupted only by an occasional exhale out of the window. But even though Lester tried he failed to see any connection between what his friend was telling him and the house on Ocean Avenue. "So what's all that got to do with Amityville?" he finally asked.

"They're both scenes of famous crimes, stupid," Kooch explained.

"Oh," Lester grunted. He let his mouth hang open so his friend could inspect the enormous wad of wet, mangled gum. Then his face sobered. "So, smart guy, what makes a crime famous?"

"Newspaper and TV coverage makes it famous." Kooch still had an exasperated look on his face. "Jesus, Lester, don't you ever read anything but the sports page?"

"I was too young to read when that happened."

Kooch's "stick" had burnt down to the point that it was burning his fingers, and he flipped it out the window. "All I'm sayin'," he started to explain, "is that kind of shit is really spooky." Before he could go on his attention was diverted by a tall, bearded man standing on the street corner in front of Whistleman's Dairy Store. The man's name was Moe, and Kooch owed him money—$12.00—which he didn't have and didn't know how he was going to get. Kooch slid down in his seat again to make certain Moe didn't see him.

"That thing you're talkin' about, that guy killin' his family and all, that was a long time ago," Lester finally said. He had had a while to think about it.

"What was?" Kooch asked. He was raising up in his seat again now that they were safely past Moe.

Lester checked for the telltale sign of Mrs. Camino's searching eyes in the rearview mirror before he answered. "I'm talkin' about that haunted house back there. All that stuff happened a long time ago."

"How long ago?"

Lester wrinkled his nose. "Awww, who knows and who cares? Its been there ever since I started going to school at Saint Alomar. Its always been all boarded up like that. Last year when me and Benny Lorentz use to ride to school together we use to take turns tryin' to guess how many rats was in there."

"Rats? You dickhead, what makes you think it's full of rats?"

"Haunted houses are always full of rats." Lester grinned. "Everybody knows haunted houses are full of rats and stuff. Rats is what keep the ghosts company."

Kooch laughed, but only after Lester's wink gave away the fact that he was pulling his leg. When he did start laughing, Lester followed suit. The laughter deteriorated into a bout of pushing and shoving and continued until Lester looked up and realized that Mrs. Camino was glaring hard at them in her rearview mirror.

The boys were still giggling when the Saint Alomar bus stopped at 3257 Oak Street and Lester Chambers got off. As Lester descended the steps to the street, Mrs. Camino informed him that she would be reporting both him and Kooch Webster to Monsignor McConnell.

Following dinner that evening, Charla Webster instructed her son to take out the garbage. The garbage cans were located in the alley behind their garage. Of all his chores, Kooch hated this one the most, not because he was opposed to the task itself, but because Kooch Webster was not as brave as he pretended to be. He had to go into the alley alone—and that made a difference. The alley was dark, and Kooch was convinced that there were terrible "things" in that alley, "things" that defied description.

Only after his mother had threatened him

with the loss of the evening's television privileges did the boy muster up his courage and resign himself to his fate.

That evening, his fears were justified. Just as he was replacing the lids on the cans, a tall figure emerged from the shadows. The man's identity was concealed by the darkness, but Kooch recognized the voice.

"Did you forget about me?" the man asked.

A startled Kooch jumped backward just as the man reached out and grabbed him by the front of his shirt.

"You owe me twelve bucks, shit brains. I want it—by Saturday noon—or I come lookin' for you."

The phone rang in the Chambers house shortly after 7:30 that same evening. Lester's new stepmother answered. "Lester," she called out, "it's for you."

Lester Chambers was afraid every call was from Bryan Lightmiller, who was the only boy he knew at Saint Alomar that got poorer grades than he did. Bryan Lightmiller slept through all of his classes, and each night he called Lester to see what homework they had been assigned. Lester had once called Bryan a dink, right in front of the whole class, and Sister Bertha had come down hard on him for what she called his profanity. That was the last time Lester called anyone a dink.

"Yeah, Bryan, whatcha want this time?" Lester grumbled.

"It's me," Kooch whispered.

Despite the trouble Kooch had gotten him into, Lester was anxious to talk to his new friend. "Whatcha up to?"

"I been sittin' here thinkin' about that haunted house. What do ya suppose is in there?" Kooch had decided not to mention his encounter with Moe and the idea that had occurred to him on his way back into the house.

"I told you, rats and ghosts and slimy things that puke green stuff all over ya . . ." Lester started to giggle, but his friend didn't join in with him.

"How do ya know? You ever been inside that old dump?"

Lester was horrified at the idea. "Are you kiddin'? My dad said he'd skin me alive if I ever went near that place."

"Why?"

"Because it's haunted, I guess."

"Yeah? Well, tell me this, pecker head, how does your dad know if it's haunted if he ain't ever been in it?"

Kooch was asking him questions faster than Lester could come up with satisfactory answers. "Because."

"Because why?"

"Because he was livin' here in Amityville when all that weird stuff happened. My dad says a house is never the same after something like that happens."

Kooch Webster laughed. "Come on, Lester,

admit it, you're scared of ghosts. You actually think there's ghosts in there, don't ya?"

"Don't either," Lester lied. He wasn't about to admit to anyone, particulary Kooch, that he believed in ghosts and a wide assortment of other scary creatures.

"Well, neither do I. So you got nothin' to be afraid of if we go in there, right?"

"Hey, man, I told ya, I ain't goin' in there. It ain't worth the grief I'll get from my dad." Lester was seldom adamant about anything, but the house at 112 Ocean Avenue was one of them.

"Know what I think, Lester? I think you're chicken. You're scared. It ain't got anything to do with your old man tellin' you ya can't. You're just a big chicken."

"Am not," Lester protested. "I'd go in there, all right, if there was a reason."

"Suppose I gave you a reason."

"Like what?"

"I saw you lookin' at that stick I had on the bus today. You're dyin' to try one, and you know it."

Lester hesitated. He was curious, but curious didn't exactly mean he was dying to try one. All of the guys at school talked about smoking pot, and the way Lester viewed it, he was probably the only boy at Saint Alomar that hadn't tried it. In the final analysis, it was just one more thing that made him feel different from the rest of the kids. "Awww, I saw that tin you carry. That was your last one."

"Hey, man, I got a source. I can get more anytime I want it—for you, for me, and anybody else that wants to try it. But you gotta show me some balls first. You gotta go in that house—and I have to see you do it."

Alice May Chambers had coped with the riddles of life for over 47 years, but she had struggled with the vagaries of being a wife and mother for only two months. After 23 years of diligent toil in the service of the Poor Handmaids of Christ, Sister Mary Alice had forsaken her vows, forfeited her habit and left the order to pursue the pleasures of the secular life. The problem was that there had been very few pleasures, and she often regretted her decision.

Then, as fate would have it, she met Roy Chambers at the monthly Catholic singles party in the basement of the church at Saint Alomar.

Alice May was well aware of statistics that indicate the longer a woman remains single the less likely it is that she will marry. She was even more aware that the chances of a woman finding a husband after the age of 40 were virtually nil. Her story was all the more remarkable, because she had passed that fortieth milestone plus seven and was not, by her own admission, attractive.

A frail woman with sharp, birdlike features and lacking in color, she suffered from a conglomeration of maladies that made her appear to be both overly somber and preoccupied with her miseries. She was, according to the assessments in her personnel files still on record with the Order, "high-strung and frequently anxious." Alice May, as well as the people who knew her, shared the belief that she had been rescued from her life of loneliness and disappointment by the widowed Roy Chambers for no other reason than he needed a mother for his two children.

Despite these apparent shortcomings, Alice May was both gentle and loving. In addition, she was determined to fill the maternal void left by the untimely death of Roy Chambers' first wife. From the outset, she had determined that the quickest way to be assimilated into her ready-made family was to focus on her role as a mother.

On this particular evening, she looked up from her never-ending labors over her personal journal and consoled herself with the fact that her hard-working husband was sleeping soundly. She could hear him snoring in the next room. Her marriage, much to her dismay, was not the physical and loving relationship she had hoped it would be.

Alice May had known Roy Chambers for all of five months prior to accepting his proposal of marriage. He was, in fact, industrious, honest and a devout Roman Catholic, but he was not the loving and tender father that she had believed him to be prior to their marriage. In the short time that they had been married, Alice May discovered that her husband was often unreasonable and frequently imposed overly severe disciplinary measures on the younger of his two children, his son, Lester. After two months of marriage, Alice May was still unable to determine the reason for her husband's frequent displays of hostility toward the boy. By the same token, she was equally convinced that Lester was unaware of his father's antagonistic feelings toward him.

Also, Alice May was saddled with a new concern. His name was Donald Webster, but Lester called him Kooch. She knew very little about the Webster boy aside from the fact that he and his mother, a recently divorced woman by the name of Charla, had moved out to the island from Brooklyn sometime during the summer. Beyond that, her information was sketchy, except for one important piece of information. Donald Webster had been seen purchasing drugs in front of Whistleman's Dairy Store. Saul Whistleman had confirmed as much, having twice spotted the boy making his purchases in front of his store.

Alice May was also aware that Lester and Donald Webster had become very close friends in a very short period of time. To Alice May's always cautious way of thinking, it was much too close and much too quick. Added now to these concerns was the conversation she had overheard earlier that evening. The two boys had openly talked about going into the old house on Ocean Avenue, a place that Roy Chambers repeatedly had reminded his son was off-limits.

For the record, Alice May Chambers' journal would indicate that she was not the kind of person who put stock in talk of such things as hauntings, ghosts and poltergeists. She was, however, a God-fearing woman, fully convinced of the presence of evil and the existence of malicious forces. Elsewhere in her journal she openly stated that she had never actually encountered a demon during her 47 years, but she did believe that satanic forces were fully capable of presenting themselves as such. The entry in her journal on this particular date is the first indication of her evolving concern that evil forces were present in this situation.

She wrote, *"I find these recollections disturbing. Although the events occurred several years ago, they are still all too vivid in my mind."*

What Alice May Chambers was referring to was the hysterical behavior of one Pierre Client, a classmate of one of the Lutz children. She recalled that the Client boy was inconsolable the day Sister Mary Margaret escorted him from the school to the mother house, babbling incoherently about a thick, green slime that began oozing suddenly from the Lutz child's book in study hall. Young Client was first left in her care, then sent home, and the incident was all but forgotten—forgotten, that is, until the story of what happened at 112 Ocean Avenue began to unfold to the rest of the tiny Amityville community.

Now, Alice May's new son was being tempted to explore that same abandoned old house and the "vehicle of his temptation" (her words) was a youngster the woman would describe in the subsequent pages of her journal as a "paladin of evil."

Her journal entry for that date also indicated that she intended to seek guidance on the matter through prayer.

AUTHOR'S NOTE: THERE IS NOTHING IN JOHN KELLY'S FILES TO INDICATE THAT ANY OF THE PRINCIPALS, WITH THE EXCEPTION OF ALICE MAY CHAMBERS, AS REMOTE AS THAT CONTACT MAY HAVE BEEN, HAD ANY PRIOR CONTACT WITH EITHER THE LUTZ FAMILY OR THE HOUSE ON OCEAN AVENUE.

THE READER WILL ALSO DISCOVER, AS I DID, A NUMBER OF REFERENCES TO EVENTS ABOUT WHICH THEY HAVE NO PRIOR KNOWLEDGE. I CAN ONLY ASSUME, SINCE WE HAVE NO WAY OF KNOWING FOR CERTAIN, THAT ALICE MAY CHAMBERS SAW SOME CONNECTION BETWEEN THOSE OCCURRENCES AND THE EVENTS THAT ARE DESCRIBED IN THE PAGES THAT FOLLOW.

. . . DAY TWO . . .

Lester Chambers and Kooch Webster did not board the Saint Alomar Academy bus that afternoon. Monsignor McConnell collared them just as they were leaving Sister McMurtry's geography class after the last bell. Monsignor David McConnell was feared by the students of Saint Alomar, although, according to Lester, he was less feared than Sister Bertha. McConnell, 60, was a bitter and humorless little man with chipmunk cheeks and lifeless brown eyes that appeared to be fixed in a permanent squint. He was short, overweight and not at all impressive, not much taller in many cases than the students he frequently confronted. But because he was a Monsignor, he had the awesome authority of Mother Church on his side.

"Mrs. Camino tells me you two are having trouble maintaining the proper decorum on the bus," he snarled.

Lester wasn't exactly certain what the word "decorum" meant, but he assumed it had something to do with smoking. He wanted to tell the Monsignor he wasn't guilty and that Kooch was the real sinner, but he knew that if he did, it would be the end of his friendship with Kooch. Rather than say anything, he looked down at the marble flooring to avoid McConnell's angry glare.

"Aw, she's lyin'," Kooch charged. "We wasn't doin' anythin'." Unlike Lester, Kooch took McConnell's charge to mean that the bus driver had reported them for pushing and shoving. To Kooch's way of thinking, the Camino woman probably hadn't even seen him smoking. He was always careful and had smoked on the bus dozens of times without getting caught, so why this time?

Lester stared back at the bulbous, balding head protruding above the tight Roman collar, convinced that Kooch was well on his way to getting thrown out of school. The Monsignor had long been noted for his quick temper, and Lester had heard terrible stories about kids getting expelled for talking back.

"This place is crawlin' with dumb rules," Kooch complained.

Lester winced.

"Oh, so now they're dumb rules, are they?" an angry McConnell repeated. Lester knew that

THE NIGHTMARE CONTINUES

Kooch didn't even see the blow coming. McConnell slapped him across the mouth and grabbed him by the shoulder, forcing him to his knees. "That's where you belong, Donald Webster, on your knees, praying—praying that you learn to keep that smart mouth of yours shut."

Lester was all but forgotten. Kooch had become the total focus of the man's anger, and Lester watched as the enraged Monsignor doled out a penance of ten rosaries, to be said aloud, there, on his knees on that very spot.

While Kooch began reciting the string of "Hail Marys" and "Our Fathers," McConnell turned his wrath on Lester.

"And you, young man, don't think your father isn't going to hear about this episode. I want him to know about your reprehensible behavior and just what kind of people you're running around with."

Lester tried hard to squeeze back the tears. Monsignor McConnell's shouting had drawn a crowd of students, and Lester did not want them to see him crying.

By the time Kooch had finished his lengthy act of contrition, Mrs. Camino and her bus had departed, leaving the boys to face a two mile trek home. While Lester bemoaned his misfortune and his impending confrontation with his father, Kooch fumed, plotting ways to get back at the priest for his humiliation. It wasn't until the boys turned onto Ocean Avenue that Kooch's disposition began to brighten.

"Hey, look, we're goin' right past that old house. This is your chance."

"Chance for what?"

"To prove you're not chicken."

Lester grimaced. "Awww, come on, Kooch, you're not startin' that stuff again. We're in enough trouble already. My dad's gonna pound on me for sure—and all because you had to mouth off and smoke on the bus. Hey, McConnell might even expel us."

Kooch stopped walking and glared at his friend. "Know what, Lester? You're turnin' out to be a real candy ass. I saw you bawlin' back there in the hall. First, you turn chicken, and now you're a crybaby. Don't ya see, McConnell is bluffin'. Old fart face ain't gonna expel us because he can't afford to. He won't throw us out because the school needs the money too much. My old man told me he has to give my mom an extra twenty-five hundred dollars a year just for me to go to Saint Alomar. Them nuns and them priests need that tuition money. No way are they gonna expel us."

"Yeah, but . . ." Lester wanted to protest, but Kooch made sense; he had heard his own father complain about the high cost of sending him to a private Catholic school.

While Lester was still trying to sort it all out, Kooch repeated his charge. "I still say you're a chicken if you don't go in there."

Lester was starting to waver. "How far in?"

"All you gotta do is go in the house, go upstairs and signal from a second floor window.

30

When you do that I'll know you're not a chicken and you get a stick. Deal?"

Kooch reached in his pocket and hauled out his battered water-stained snuff can. It was identical to the one Moe used, except, of course, Kooch had retrieved his from a trash can in the alley behind Joe Phillips' house. He opened it, gave Lester a glimpse of the prize and shoved it back in his pocket.

In a way, Kooch had outsmarted himself; the action was just a little too quick for Lester. He was tempted, but with all his problems, he wasn't sure it was worth it. "I don't think I wanta'." For Lester, there were two problems. The first was his uncertainty about the whole subject of pot; he wanted to try it, to be one of the guys, but he was afraid to. The second had to do with his father. What if Monsignor McConnell did tell his father he had been smoking on the bus? Lester reasoned that if he didn't smoke one of Kooch's "sticks" in the first place, he could honestly tell his dad he had never smoked, thus avoiding a lie and having to admit either of his sins in the confessional. For Lester, he was exhibiting unusual logic.

Still, if he didn't go into the house, he knew that Kooch would use it against him. It was bad enough that Kooch saw him crying. Now Kooch was calling him chicken. If Kooch started telling the kids at school that Lester was afraid to try pot, it would be almost as bad as his dad getting a call from Monsignor.

"All I have to do is signal from the second floor window?"

"That's all. Do it and you get a nail."

"Yeah, but—how am I gonna' get in?"

"Hey, man, that's your problem."

"I thought you told me last night that we were goin' in together," Lester suddenly reminded him.

"I ain't the one that's got anything to prove," Kooch sneered.

Lester knew he had run out of ways to stall. He started up the drive, then slowly circled the house, studying it from every angle. The inspection even included the garage, the empty swimming pool and the delapitated old boathouse that fronted on the Amityville River. The outbuildings were boarded up and locked which was encouraging—maybe the house would be locked, too. Finally he tried the doors, front and back, and breathed a sigh of relief; they were locked, too.

He walked back down the driveway with a swagger and managed a whistle. He had tried. "Ain't no way in. Everything's locked."

"I know a way." Kooch grinned and pointed to one of the basement windows along the drive. "Just kick it in."

"But that's against the law," Lester protested. "Didn't ya see the signs? They're all over the place. 'No Trespassing.'"

Kooch walked up the drive, selected a window, planted himself firmly on the concrete surface and cocked his knees. One thrust was all it took. He kicked out the rotted wood casing, and shards of broken glass clattered to the floor inside. "There, dickhead, now you got a way in."

Lester stared into the darkness beyond the opening and swallowed hard. He was trapped. Kooch had him. There was no way to save face and not go in. He lay down on his stomach and poked his head in the opening to look around. It was even worse than he had feared. Beyond was a world of pitch-black and foul odors. His eyes began to tear, and he backed out.

Kooch was snickering. "See, I knew you'd turn chicken." He pulled out his snuff tin, extracted one of the loosely wrapped joints and lit it. Then he slumped back against the side of the house and tried to twist his face into a look of ecstasy. Much later, Lester would learn that Kooch had no intention of sharing anything more than a drag with Lester. Until Kooch was able to come up with the money to pay Moe, his supply was shut off—and that was only half of his problem with Moe.

"How about a puff for me?" Lester pleaded. He had heard the kids tell how it made them brave, and it occurred to him that just one drag might give him the courage he needed to crawl through the window."

"No way. When I see the signal, you get the stick."

AUTHOR'S NOTE: MUCH OF WHAT WE KNOW ABOUT THIS INCIDENT LESTER REVEALED TO HIS STEPMOTHER IN A TEARFUL CON-

FESSION THAT EVENING. IT APPEARS HE HELD NOTHING BACK, AND ALICE MAY CHAMBERS PROVED TO BE BOTH A COMPETENT AND COMPULSIVE CHRONICLER OF THESE EVENTS, RECORDING MUCH OF WHAT LESTER TOLD HER VERBATIM.

Suddenly, Lester appeared to accept his fate. To Kooch's astonishment, he turned around, poked his legs through the opening and began to lower himself through the window.

When Lester dropped to the floor, he found himself in a dirt-crusted, foul-smelling world where the stench of pent-up mildew and decay choked him. His only source of light was the last vestige of day checkering in through the broken window.

He scrambled to his feet, peered into the blackness and tried to get his bearings. Knowing he was next to the wall, he put out his hand to steady himself, cautiously running the other hand along the coarse surface in the hope that there would be a light switch that worked.

He took a step and stumbled, got up and stumbled again. The floor of the room was cluttered with debris. Lester was trying hard not to let his imagination run away with him. Even so, he had visions of things so unspeakable crouching in the vile blackness that he knew he would never live long enough to tell anyone about them.

Still, if this was a basement similar to the one

in the house he lived in, there had to be a stairway up to the first floor. No house, he told himself, not even a haunted house, had a basement without having stairs. He took a step forward, ran his hand along the wall again and felt something wet and slimy. His hand recoiled, his heart pounded, and a series of chills raced up his back. He was terrified—more terrified than he had ever been in his whole life. In the clawing darkness there was nothing but confusion and clutter, and his senses were bombarded by mind-bending images and gut-wrenching stenches. Lester was positive he was going to throw up at any minute.

He gathered himself, took a step away from the wall and groped in front of him. Another step—and then another. Each time he stumbled. The floor was littered with God knows what—maybe even the bodies of the people that guy had killed. He was sweating. His breath was coming out in short, loud puffs, and he could feel his knees shaking. Lester told himself that if he could just get out of this alive, he vowed he would never cuss again, that he would go to Mass every day and study his catechism until he knew every line by heart.

Suddenly his hand came in contact with a heavy piece of smooth angular wood. His fingers traced along the surface until they started up. He had found it. He was elated. It was the railing on the steps. This was it—it had to be. But what if some of the steps were missing? What if he started up and fell through? Not only that, suppose he got all the way to the top and the door wouldn't open? Then what? Would he have to come back down and work his way back across this stinking, scary basement again? Even if he could make it back to the window, how would he get out? He knew he couldn't heft himself back through the small opening. Why did it suddenly seem darker? What had happened to the daylight coming in through the window? What was Kooch doing?

The tears welled up again and began to trickle down his face.

He clutched the railing and slowly began working his way around until he was facing the steps. He tried the first one; it held. He tried the second one, and it too held.

The third step creaked, and his knees began shaking again.

The fourth step buckled. He heard the sound of splintering wood and felt it give way. He fell, plunging face first into a tangle of whatever God-awful thing ghosts stored under their basement stairwell. Then he screamed for help; if nothing else it proved he was still alive.

He lay there for several minutes, praying, trying to regulate his breathing, gulping for air. He was entangled in things that smelled so terrible and so awful his fevered brain wouldn't allow him to think about them. What if this was the place where the murderer threw the body parts like arms and legs and even severed heads?

Something trickled down over his lip, something wet and warm. He tried to smear it away and felt the substance cling to his hand. It was on his lips—salty, thick and sticky. A nosebleed? That was it—a nosebleed; he had them all the time, sometimes for no reason at all.

But what if it wasn't a nosebleed? What if it was something else? Worse yet, what if it was someone else's blood?

He clawed his way out of the tangle, reached up and got a grip on the first step above the one that had broken. He pulled on it; it seemed strong, strong enough to support him. He had to get to that door, and he had to get it open fast. Kooch's dumb old pot was no longer the issue; getting out of there alive was.

This time, on all fours, he made it all the way to the top. He reached up, grabbed the knob, twisted it and watched the door slowly creak open. The grey filtered light of the long-closeted house spilled over him, and he could see again.

He had emerged in the hallway. It looked like a war zone—litter and trash, broken glass, turned over furniture, empty cartons, everything he expected except the rats. He had forgotten all about the rats. They were probably down there in the basement with him. In fact, they were probably right there with him in that pile of trash and ghost stuff. The more he thought about it, the more he began to tremble. When he felt the warm, wet sensation, he knew it was too late. He looked down, and even in the grim half-light of the hour, he could see the telltale wet stain creeping down from his crotch.

Lester sat nervously on an old chair with his legs crossed, praying that the encroaching darkness would hide his embarrassment. He had opened the back door to let Kooch in. Now Kooch was threading his way from room to room, inspecting a world of blotted and cracked plaster walls, soot-stained woodwork and furnishings heavy with the pungent odor of rot. It was a world of somber, deathlike colorlessness. What little light that was left of the day was being shut out by the heavy folds of rotting drapes.

Kooch walked back into the room. "Looks about like I thought it would. But now that I see all this stuff I got an even better idea."

"What kind of idea?"

"Tell you about it on the way home," Kooch promised. "Let's blow this joint."

Lester followed his friend down the hall to the door at the rear of the house. As Kooch stepped out on the porch, Lester started to pull the door shut behind him. That was when he heard it. It was, he thought, a woman's voice. It said, "Don't come back."

Lester jerked the door shut, heard it slam and raced back down the driveway toward the street. He didn't stop until his chest hurt too much to continue. Several minutes later, Kooch caught up with him.

"Hey, dickhead, whatcha runnin' for?"

"Gotta get home," Lester said. On the spur of the moment Lester, who tried not to lie because he believed it was a sin, told Kooch that he had just remembered he was supposed to go somewhere with his father that evening and that when he looked at his watch he realized he was already late. He did not tell Kooch about the voice or that he had wet his pants. If Kooch knew either, Lester knew he would never let him forget it.

"All I wanted to tell you," Kooch said, "is that you've got some kind of black shit all over you. It's on your jacket, and you've got it on your hand."

It was shortly after six o'clock when Roy Chambers arrived home from work. The ritual in the Chambers house called for everyone to meet in the foyer of the two-story house and greet the family breadwinner. From there they would retire to the family room for 15 minutes or so of small talk, and then Alice Chambers would return to the kitchen to continue preparing supper.

On this occasion, even though Mr. Chambers was later than usual, Lester had not yet arrived home from school. Chambers inquired as to the boy's whereabouts.

Neither Alice May nor his sister, Ellen, knew —but Mrs. Chambers had her suspicions. Those suspicions presented Roy Chambers' new wife with something of a quandary. She had overheard the telephone conversation between her stepson and the Webster boy. If she reasoned correctly, Donald Webster had probably talked Lester into stopping at 112 Ocean Avenue.

Before Roy Chambers had the opportunity to press the issue, the door opened and Lester walked in. His pants were torn, he was dirty, and there was a large, oily, black stain on his jacket.

"Where have you been?" Roy Chambers growled.

Lester, never one to challenge authority, spewed out his story. "Monsignor McConnell gave us detention for misbehaving on the school bus yesterday. By the time we was through, the bus was gone, and we had to walk."

Ellen Chambers, quick to take advantage of any situation where her brother might be in trouble, pointed out that it did not take three hours to walk home from Saint Alomar.

Defensive, Lester promptly launched into a lengthy description of how he and Kooch had decided to try to make up for lost time by taking the deserted spur bridge across the Amityville River. Then he described how he had fallen between trestle supports, which, he claimed, accounted for the unsightly black smear on his clothes and skin.

Older than Lester by two years, Ellen was enjoying her brother's obvious discomfort. She stood behind Roy Chambers and made faces at her brother. Disappointed when their father failed to pick up on the detention issue, she followed Lester upstairs when the boy was instructed to get cleaned up for dinner.

THE NIGHTMARE CONTINUES

While Lester attempted to remove the stain on the back of his hand with a variety of soaps and cleansers, Ellen watched.

"I wonder," she teased, "just what would happen if Alice and me called your buddy, Kooch? Why is it I get the feeling we wouldn't get the same story you just told Dad?"

"Go ahead and call him." Lester was confident. The two boys had carefully rehearsed their story on the way home.

"It all sounds pretty dumb to me, Lester. If you're gonna start lying to Dad, you better learn to come up with something more believable. That part about falling between the trestles sounded pretty stupid, too. If I'd been doing something I wasn't supposed to, I'd at least have come up with a story that wasn't so dumb."

Lester knew Ellen was baiting him. He had learned early on not to depend on her. Because of that, they shared few, if any, brother-sister secrets. There were occasions when they did not speak to each other for days.

"Now, tell me what really happened," she whispered as she entered the room and closed the door.

"I told you what happened." Lester was certainly quick enough to realize that, well-thought-out or not, he was stuck with his story.

Ellen was not the thorn in her brother's side that she believed she was. For the most part, Lester knew how to control her. He did it with a combination of bribes, threats and menacing looks. He had never actually hit her because he figured that, in the long run, it would end up hurting him more than it did her, but—and he admitted as much to his stepmother on several occasions—there were times when he wanted to.

"Can't ya see I'm busy. Go away and leave me alone."

Making no headway on the stain, he reached under the cabinet for a can of scouring powder. As he did, something fell out of his pocket. Ellen swooped down and picked it up before he could. "It's a belt. Where'd you get it?"

"Found it. Now give it back."

Ellen rolled it over in her hands and examined the jeweled buckle with the scarred crest. She could make out the initial "R" but the other two initials were impossible to identify.

"Found it where?" she taunted.

Lester snatched the belt out of her hands and crammed it back in his pocket. "None of your business." He picked up the cleanser and began rubbing on the stain again.

"You've been up to something," Ellen insisted. She leaned forward and smelled his breath. "You've been smoking. I knew you'd been up to something."

Lester's face turned a vivid crimson. "So?"

"Wait till Dad hears about this," Ellen threatened.

Lester was flustered. He only had taken two drags off of one of Kooch's sticks. He didn't tell Kooch, but the sweet, pungent taste had almost made him gag. "Big deal, so I took a couple of drags."

"Yeah, but I know what kind of stuff your buddy smokes. Old Mr. Whistleman told Alice he saw that creepy friend of yours buying pot from Moe Williams."

Now he was really rattled. Lester resorted to the only weapon he had left. Being bigger than his sister, he grabbed her by the arm and shoved her back against the bathroom wall. "Look, Ellen, I'm warnin' ya—one word about this to Dad and I'll tell him about you and that black guy you been messin' around with after school." Kooch had heard about Ellen through one of his buddies at Saint Alomar, and he in turn had told Lester. Lester, more cunning than usual, had been saving this juicy tidbit for a time such as this—a time when he really needed it. Roy Chambers hated blacks, so much so that he refused to let Lester try out for the Academy's CYO League football team because, by doing so, Lester would be associating with the black kids on the team.

For the moment, he had her. Ellen backed off, but he knew his victory would be short-lived. He had to come up with something better, something more permanent. Ellen had two weak spots, greed and vanity, and Lester knew how to manipulate her weaknesses.

He pushed his face up close to hers and lowered his voice to make certain no one could hear him. "Look, keep your mouth shut and maybe there could be something in this for you, too."

Ellen was hooked—but cautious. "Just tell me what you're up to, bonehead. I'll decide for myself."

"Me and Kooch broke into that old house on Ocean Avenue."

"The haunted one?" But before Lester could confirm it, her expression eroded into one of skepticism. "Nawww," she drawled, "you're lyin'; you'd be afraid to go in there."

"Honest. That's where the belt came from. Kooch found it in a second floor closet. That place is full of neat stuff. It looks like whoever lived there just took off and left stuff."

"So what's in for me?"

"Here's the deal. You keep your mouth shut about what me and Kooch are doin', and I keep quiet about you and your friend. Plus—I bring you somethin' from that old house."

"Like what?"

Lester released her arm and started working on the stain again. "Hey," he said, mocking Kooch, "just tell me what you want."

"You say they just took off and left everything behind? Even their jewelry?"

"Even jewelry," Lester lied. It was his second lie within the hour. At the rate he was going, Lester figured Monsignor McConnell would have him saying penance for a whole week.

"Just bring me something; then I'll let you know whether we got a deal or not."

Lester let out a sigh of relief. He had bought

himself some time. The moral issue of stealing things from a house where nobody lived was a matter he would deal with later. He wondered how many years a man had to spend in purgatory for stealing things from an abandoned house. By making his deal with Ellen, he was betting that purgatory wasn't as bad as his dad knowing about him breaking into that old house or smoking pot.

He backed away from the girl, opened the door and let her out. Then he closed the door again and started working on the stain again.

Six blocks away, Kooch Webster was examining the items he had stolen from the house on Ocean Avenue. There was a flashlight, a pocket knife, a matching pen and pencil set bearing the name of a construction company on the box and an old Bulova watch. Neither the flashlight nor the watch worked.

After assessing them, he began to think about other possibilities he had seen scattered about the place. For Kooch, things were working out even better than he had hoped. He picked up the phone and called Lester.

"It's me, Kooch. Did ya get in any trouble?"

"Naw," Lester said, "not really. My dad bought that bit about the old spur bridge."

Kooch was far too excited to let Lester drone on about something that was already a given and cut him off. "Hey, man, you never did tell me what you thought of the pop; you just handed it back." Moe called them nails, pops and sticks.

Kooch had learned he could even sound like Moe when he put his mind to it. He practiced walking and talking like Moe in front of the mirror when he was alone.

"It was okay, I guess."

"Okay? Is that all?" It wasn't as much enthusiasm as Kooch had hoped for. Kooch reasoned that if he couldn't get Lester to buy sticks from him, then Lester wouldn't need the money—and if Lester didn't need the money, he might not be willing to go along with the scheme. "That ain't the reason I called ya. What I really called for is—I got a great idea for how me and you can make some money."

Lester was only half-listening. He was preoccupied with the stain. Even a liberal application of Ellen's hydrogen peroxide hadn't dented it. "How?"

"Me and you could sell some of that stuff laying around that old house." When Lester didn't respond, Kooch decided to lay out his plan in detail. "This is what we do. We walk home everyday instead of riding the bus. We stop at the house, carry out a couple of things each day, stash 'em in the garage, and on Saturday we take 'em down to Silverman's pawnshop. We tell him some old lady hired us to clean out her garage and said we could have anything we carried out."

Kooch was still waiting for Lester's response when he heard a woman's scream. It came from Lester's end of the line. Then he heard the hollow clanging sound of the phone hitting the floor.

When Lester got to the basement he found his stepmother cowering in the corner. The woman's face was twisted in terror, and she was sobbing. The clothes hamper was tipped over, and soiled clothes were strewn about her. In the far corner of the room, hissing and pulsating like some kind of fearful, mortally wounded animal, was Lester's leather jacket. To Lester it appeared to be breathing. The black oily stain that had been only on the sleeve now saturated the entire garment. A hazy, blue-gray, foul-smelling vapor hovered over it like a demonic mist devouring its prey.

Lester jumped back just as Ellen and his father rushed down. Like him, they stood watching, too terrified to move.

Alice Chambers would record in her journal: *"Whatever it was, it appeared to be devouring itself."*

. . . DAY THREE . . .

Because of pressing financial obligations inherited from her late husband, Sara Wine held down two jobs. By day she was a truant officer for the local school district, and at night she was a dispatcher for the county sheriff. She was on her way to work at the school administration building when she stopped at the Suffolk County police station. On her way into the station she encountered Lt. Jerome Steinberg coming up the walk. Sara Wine knew the homicide officer, having been introduced to him at a recent police seminar.

After a few pleasantries, she handed Steinberg a brown paper sack containing an assortment of textbooks. "Do me a favor, Jerry, and give these to whoever handles stuff like this. I'm running late."

Curious, Steinberg peered into the sack. "What are they?"

"Oh, just some school books. We got a call from a couple up on Ocean Avenue last night. They claimed some kids were playing around over at the old Lutz place. We dispatched a unit, but by the time we got there they were gone. All we found were these books."

"What were they doing?"

Sara shrugged. "Who knows? All we could find was a busted window."

Steinberg shook his head. "Wish to hell someone would tear that old place down."

"If they did, this town would lose its main tourist attraction," Sara said, laughing. She glanced at her watch and started back down the steps. "Well, do whatever it is you do with stuff like this, but I do think somebody should call the kids' parents and warn them to keep their kids away from that place. One of these days, someone is going to get hurt over there."

Promising to take care of the matter, Steinberg watched Sara get in her car, then went into the station. He handed the sack to the desk sergeant. "Have somebody drop these off over at Saint Alomar, and tell whoever takes them to chew out the kids that lost them. One of the sheriff's deputies found these out at the old Lutz place last night."

"I thought that old dump was posted."

"Damn right it's posted, but you know how kids are. You'd think the kids would have enough sense to stay away from it."

"Hell, Jerry, most of the kids over at Saint Alomar weren't even born yet the last time we had trouble over there."

Alice May Chambers spent a mostly sleepless night after the incident in the basement.

Ellen, likewise, had been difficult to console. Alice May had stayed with the girl in her room until she finally slipped into a fitful sleep.

Lester was less emotional about the bizarre occurrence but did seem troubled and withdrawn. Alice May noted in her journal that Lester went to bed without being told—a first since she had assumed her new duties.

Roy Chambers, following the incident in the basement, helped his wife remove the residue of the burnt garment and put it in a trash can in the alley behind the house. The odor lingered, however, and he arranged two fans in the basement and opened the windows to help dissipate it. He then retired to his reading room, an unused bedroom on the second floor, and closed the door.

At that point, Alice retired to her button room to write in her journal.

Her diary for the 14th day of October would seem to indicate that she began to record the earlier event with the jacket and then decided to talk to her son before he went to sleep. After what turned out to be a lengthy conversation with the boy, she returned to her room and continued her writing. The entry appears to be a near verbatim recounting of their talk:

"He was quite surprised that I was able to perceive how upset he was. When I entered his room, it was drafty and quite cold, yet Lester was sweating profusely. I asked him if he wanted to talk about what happened earlier.

"At first he was reluctant to discuss it, but after I bathed his forehead with a cool, damp cloth, he began to relax and soon the story came out.

"He told me how he and Donald Webster had broken into the house on Ocean Avenue and how his friend had taken a number of items from the house. He also confessed that the black stain had resisted all of his efforts to get rid of it. Then he revealed that the stain did not come from a fall on the railroad trestle as he first told us, but happened sometime when he fell in the basement of the house.

"He also mentioned a voice that spoke harshly to him as he was leaving the old house. I did not press the issue because he seemed confused and frightened. His greatest concern, however, still appears to be that he has disappointed his father by disobeying him.

"I suggested that he could find solace in prayer. Then I held his hand, and we prayed. Soon after, he fell asleep."

AUTHOR'S NOTE: FROM THE MANNER IN WHICH ALICE CHAMBERS' JOURNAL ENTRY IS CONCLUDED, IT SEEMS EVIDENT THAT SHE INTENDED TO STOP THERE. THE ENTRY IS DATED AND INITIALED, BUT A NUMBER OF CHAOTIC NOTATIONS FOLLOWED. MOST OF THEM ARE DISJOINTED PHRASES; SEVERAL WERE MERELY SCRAWLED, MEANINGLESS JUMBLES OF LETTERS. IT APPEARS THAT MRS. CHAMBERS AROSE SEVERAL TIMES DURING THE COURSE OF THE NIGHT TO MAKE ENTRIES.

ONE OBVIOUSLY ANGUISHED NOTE THAT THE READER WILL FIND CURIOUS SAYS SIMPLY, "WASH AWAY THE SIN." THE QUESTION ARISES—WAS ALICE CHAMBERS REFERRING TO LESTER'S BEHAVIOR AS THE SIN, OR WAS SHE REFERRING TO THE STAIN? THERE IS EVIDENCE OF TRADITIONAL CATHOLIC THINKING THROUGHOUT THE CHAMBERS DIARY, AND THERE IS UNCERTAINTY AS TO WHETHER SHE WAS MORE CONCERNED ABOUT THE MORAL IMPLICATIONS OF LESTER'S BEHAVIOR OR THE EXISTENCE OF THE STAIN.

ONE THING IS CERTAIN, HOWEVER. ALICE MAY CHAMBERS DID NOT SLEEP WELL THAT NIGHT.

THE NIGHTMARE CONTINUES

October 15th dawned cold and gray. The mild Indian summer weather that had preceded it for the past several days was gone. When Roy Chambers left for work that morning, there was a depressing aura about the day with overcast skies and frequent rain showers. By the time Lester and Ellen left for school (Ellen attended Saint Agnes School for Girls) the weather had further eroded with blustery winds and rain squalls.

In the Chambers household, Alice May made a brief note in her journal relative to the weather and then set about her duties. It was Friday, the day on which she went to the market in the morning and stopped by the church in the afternoon to make her weekly confession. A weekly confession assured Alice of being in a state of grace, required for Holy Communion at Mass on Sunday.

In the Webster house, Charla Webster had decided to call her office and tell them she would not be in. She told her immediate supervisor that she was ill. She gave no other explanation, nor did she speculate on when she would be in. After completing the call, she fixed herself a cup of coffee, took two Librium capsules and stared out the window at the gloomy day. Charla was feeling sorry for herself. She was depressed, and she had a hangover.

Recently divorced from her husband Merle, a newspaper reporter, Charla had expressed a certain amount of melancholy about her upcoming fortieth birthday. She was an attractive woman from an upper middle-class, Long Island family. She had graduated from law school at Columbia and was employed as a contract administrator for a large, New York-based, multinational. Her widowed mother, Mrs. Jacalyn Cordes, lived in Amityville.

Charla viewed her recent move to Amityville as the long-term solution to a number of problems. Just prior to her divorce, a promotion had elevated her to a job that required frequent overnight travel and demanded more of her time. The proximity to her mother made it possible for Jacalyn Cordes to help take care of Donald and at the same time enabled Charla to keep an eye on her mother. Jacalyn Cordes, 63, was in poor health.

For the past two months, Charla had been seeing a man from the company's audit department. As recently as the previous weekend, she had spent two days with him in Vermont. During the course of that weekend, the man informed Charla that he was married.

Brooding and distraught, Charla began drinking heavily shortly after her return from the weekend. At lunch, on Thursday, she had become inebriated and culminated the day by getting sick in her office. A colleague had brought her home, where she had gone to bed and not talked to Donald. When she awoke the following morning, she went to check on her son but found he had already left for school.

With no other plans for the day other than regaining her equalibrium, Charla returned to her son's room to examine the curious assortment of items he had left on his dresser. One by one, she inspected them. The pen and pencil set were inexpensive, promotional items from some company. The flashlight was disposable and carried the name of the same firm. The watch, however, was gold. She rolled it over in her hand and examined the well-worn casing. There was an inscription on the back, but it was obliterated to the extent that the words were indistinguishable. She could make out the word "love" and the initial "R". Beyond that, she was only guessing. Later, she would mention the watch to her mother as "unusually cold to the touch."

Around ten o'clock that morning, she phoned her mother and ask her to come over. Mrs. Cordes informed her daughter that she had a couple of errands to run but that she would be there by lunchtime.

Mrs. Cordes didn't make it to the Webster home that day. She became ill shortly after talking to her daughter and decided not to come. Alone and distraught, Charla began drinking again.

At lunch that day in the school cafeteria, Sister Mary Bertha noted the discoloration on the back of Lester's hand and inquired about it. When Lester was unable to give her a satisfactory answer about what the stain was or how he got it, Sister Bertha, fearing something contagious, took the boy to Sister Mary Alfonsa, the school nurse.

"How long have you had this?" the woman asked.

Mindful of his encounter with Monsignor McConnell the previous day, Lester was anxious to avoid any further trouble with the teachers at Saint Alomar. He repeated the story about the railroad trestle but did not tell the nurse about the jacket or breaking into the house on Ocean Avenue. Neither did he tell her that the stain appeared to be spreading. The stain was now nearly twice the size it had been the previous evening.

Sister Alfonsa used a variety of different ablutions on the stain but was unable to remove it. Noting that the nature of the stain was such that it appeared to be sensitive to the touch, she wrapped a thin layer of gauze around Lester's hand and sent him back to class.

Still concerned, Sister Alfonsa attempted to call Alice Chambers to advise the woman that she thought Lester should see a doctor. There was no answer at the Chambers house. It was Friday—when Alice May Chambers went to the market and then to confession.

Yielding to Kooch's taunts and threats, Lester waited in the boys' rest room with his friend until their school bus pulled out of the Saint Alomar courtyard without them. While the two boys walked in the rain to the house on Ocean Avenue, Kooch explained his plan to Lester.

"Yeah, but what happens if old man Silverman isn't interested in any of that junk?" Lester asked.

"No sweat. He will be. Some of that stuff is worth lots of money."

"Yeah, but suppose he ain't?" Lester pressed.

"Then I'll have to think of something else." Kooch had not told Lester about Moe's threat, and he didn't want to think about what would happen if Silverman wouldn't buy the items. At the moment, pawning the things they could steal from the house was the only plan he had to pay off Moe Williams.

Lester, on the other hand, had not told Kooch about the voice or that he had told his stepmother what actually happened the day before. "I don't think it's a very good idea."

"Why? Turnin' chicken on me again? Whatcha 'fraid of? You was in there yesterday and nothin' happened."

Lester could not tell Kooch he had promised his stepmother he wouldn't go back in the house nor could he tell him that he actually was afraid because of the voice. "I still don't think he'll buy any of that old junk," he said instead.

"It ain't junk. It's antiques we're takin' him. You know how he's always got all them antiques sittin' around his store."

Lester did not want to admit he had never been in Silverman's store; his father was as adamant about that as he was about the house on Ocean Avenue. "A boy your age has no business in a pawnshop." Roy Chambers hadn't explained why, and Lester hadn't asked.

Despite his misgivings, Lester accompanied his friend to the house and waited outside in the rain while Kooch removed a silver tea service, a large clock, some old tools and some dishes. Then Kooch broke the rusted lock on the door to the kennel and stored the items. "Hey, man, it'll work. Trust me. Tomorrow morning we get up, come over here, tell Silverman that story about cleaning out an old lady's garage, and we got money in our pockets. It's easy."

"I don't think we should," Lester stalled. Then, because he thought it would throw Kooch off his real reason for not going along with the scheme, he added, "This stuff is just junk. He ain't gonna be interested."

"Hey, man, I'll prove it to ya. We gotta go right by Silverman's place on the way home, right? We'll take him somethin' tonight. If he buys it, we're in business. Deal?"

A short time later, standing in Silverman's Pawnshop at the corner of Ewing and Comer streets, Kooch presented the pawnbroker with a set of wood augers.

Silverman lifted the antique tool out of Kooch's hand and examined it. "I'm surprised someone didn't buy this piece at your garage sale," he said. Leon Silverman knew full well that the item would have been snapped up early by the collectors if the piece had come from where the boys said it did. "And what about your friend here?" he asked, looking at Lester.

To avoid Kooch's taunts, Lester had reluctantly agreed to carry in a small dish. To Lester the bowl looked old, which logically meant that it was an antique. Lester had selected it because of the curious design in the bottom of the bowl—a cross with a chain wrapped around it. He held it out for Silverman's inspection.

Silverman frowned but did not comment. If the boys wanted him to believe the items came from a garage sale, it was all right with him. "You have more?" he asked.

"Lots," Kooch said. "You wanta see 'em?"

The old man smiled, his suspicions confirmed. "I'd like to see them," he said. "Now if you'll just give me your names, I'll make out the pawn ticket."

AUTHOR'S NOTE: SEVERAL DAYS LATER, SILVERMAN'S DAUGHTER DISCOVERED THAT PAWN TICKET. THE NAMES OF THE BOYS AND THE NUMBER OF THE AMITYVILLE POLICE DEPARTMENT HAD BEEN SCRATCHED ON THE BOTTOM OF THE TICKET. EVEN THOUGH HE MAY HAVE INTENDED TO DO SO, THERE IS NOTHING TO INDICATE LEON SILVERMAN EVER REPORTED THE INCIDENT TO THE AMITYVILLE POLICE.

Later, standing in the doorway of Carpenter's Dry Cleaners, Kooch was jubilant. Silverman had given each of them two dollars. "See, man, I told ya. It was easy; tomorrow we take him more, okay?"

Lester looked at the two crumpled one dollar bills in his gauze-covered hand. He wanted the money but did not feel right about what he had done. "Here," he said, handing the money to Kooch, "I don't want it."

Kooch looked at his friend in amazement. "Why?"

"I don't think we shoulda done that," Lester told him.

"Know somethin', Lester," Kooch sneered, "you're weird."

Leon Silverman closed his shop at precisely nine o'clock. A man of ceremony and custom, he went about the closing in the same fashion every night. He put the watches, jewels and other valuables in the safe, locked the firearms case, locked the doors, activated the security system, pulled the steel cage across the display windows, pulled down the blinds, counted the money, turned out the lights, picked up Tramaine, his cat, and exited through the rear door. His house was immediately across the alley fronting on Sixth Street. He had lived in the same house for 47 years.

For some unexplained reason, he carried the items pawned by the two boys home with him. He entered his house from the rear and placed the items on the kitchen table. He fixed a bowl of oatmeal for both himself and Tramaine, ate, washed his dishes and went upstairs to take his bath.

Following his bath, he retired to his bedroom, turned on the television to watch the ten o'clock news and quickly scanned the evening paper. At that point, he heard a noise in the hall. He left his room and started down to the first floor. He was amazed to discover the wood auger laying on the stairs.

Following her confession, Alice Chambers had stopped at the rectory to talk to Father Bellini. Father Joseph Anthony Bellini was young and the ideal assistant to the aging Monsignor McConnell. Most of the younger parishioners at Saint Alomar preferred to deal with him. Since leaving the Order, Alice had made a conscious effort to avoid McConnell. It was McConnell who had served as her Intercessor during her "period of consternation" when she decided to forfeit her habit and resign. The lengthy and difficult process had put a strain on the relationship between the two, and now, when she felt she needed the advice of someone in the Church, she sought out Father Bellini. Her question brought a smile to the young priest's face.

"How can you tell when there are evil spirits present?" he repeated. Then he laughed. "What brought all of this on?"

Alice was embarrassed but determined. She repeated her question. "I'm quite serious, Father. How can you tell?"

Bellini's laughter gave way to a perplexed frown. "Well," he stalled, trying to think of the best way to frame his response, "the Holy Mother Church does believe there are situations that indicate the actual physical presence of evil forces." His words were cautious and carefully weighed. "Why?"

Alice hesitated. What had earlier seemed like the obvious course of action, asking the priest's opinion about what had happened the previous evening, now seemed foolish.

Father Bellini tried to help her. "Even the Church recognizes the validity of certain reports about such things as ghosts and poltergeists. Are you telling me you believe you have experienced such an occurrence?"

The feeling of embarrassment persisted, but slowly she began to recount the details of what had happened the previous night in the Chambers basement. She concluded with a question. "Can you help us, Father?"

The young priest stammered for a moment before answering. Bellini's engaging smile had vanished. "I can't, Alice, but there are people in the Church who can. Would you like me to contact them on your behalf?"

"Not yet, Father," she said. Then she heard herself asking the priest if he would mind coming to the house instead.

"If it will help to put your mind at ease," he answered.

Father Joseph Bellini then agreed to stop by the Chambers house the following afternoon.

THE NIGHTMARE CONTINUES

Alice May left the rectory with the intention of recording their brief conversation in her journal.

Roy Chambers bowled in the Catholic Men's League on Friday night and usually did not arrive home until after nine o'clock. Lester's awareness of his father's Friday night routine may account for his willingness to accompany Kooch to Silverman's store and chance being late for dinner a second night in a row.

Ellen, although still somewhat upset over the disturbing scene in the basement the night before, asked for and received permission to stay overnight at a friend's house.

Alice May was in her button room writing in her journal when Lester arrived home that evening at 6:30. When the boy went immediately to his room, his stepmother went to check on him. She inquired about the stain on his hand when she saw the gauze wrapping applied by Sister Alfonsa, but Lester informed her that it appeared to be going away.

Lester had lied. The ugly stain was increasing in size and had actually started to spread between his fingers. During his shower, Lester scrubbed the stain vigorously with a brush, but despite his efforts, the stain was in no way diminished.

Following her visit with Father Bellini in the Saint Alomar rectory, Alice had stopped at the public library and obtained two books. The first was by a professor from North Carolina who worked for the Academy of Parapsychology in upstate New York. The second was authored by Bishop Harlan Jacquess of the Saint Alban Parapsychology Society. In the Jacquess book she found what she was looking for—a detailed account of an incident cited during a lecture heard in her days at the novitiate.

According to church authorities, a young girl in New Rochelle, New York, in 1957 was determined to be possessed by evil forces. Psychics and mediums from a number of prestigious and reputable parapsychological institutions investigated the case. For a period of five weeks, the girl/demon defied all attempts to exorcise the evil spirits from her body, and while her horrified parents looked on, she consumed herself by turning herself into a human torch. As the inferno raged, an oily, black residual was formed. Everyone in the room—the girl's parents, a priest and two observers from the Center for Psychic Research—died within a 24 month period. Because of the unusual events surrounding their deaths and their involvement with the so-called New Rochelle Witch, autopsies were performed. In each case, the lungs of the dead person were found to be full of an oily black substance. In effect, all of them had drowned.

In a footnote, Alice found what she was looking for and copied it verbatim in her journal:

"It has been confirmed that all five individuals were at the bedside of Elaine Cul-

bertson when she died. At one time or another during the investigation that followed, each of the individuals recalled being splattered by the substance spewing from the girl's burning body."

Alice May finished the entry in her journal and began to pray. Before long, the precise orderliness of her prayer eroded into hysterical and terrified sobs.

Leon Silverman awoke in the middle of the night, listening to strange sounds emanating from the first floor. He got out of bed, put on his robe and went down to check on the disturbance. There was a whirling sound coming from the kitchen. When he turned on the lights, he was amazed to see the antique auger standing on its tip, attempting to bore a hole in the top of the cabinet. As he stood there, the action ceased, and the tool lay gently over on its side.

Amazed and thinking that it was altogether likely he had been dreaming, he walked over and picked up the instrument. The drill tip was warm. Then he remembered that after finding the tool laying on the stairs leading to the second floor, he had put it on the back porch along with the bowl.

How had it gotten from the porch to the kitchen counter? Silverman was baffled. When he recounted these events to his doctor the next day, Dr. Malcom Eddington advised Silverman that he was probably working too hard and putting in too many hours. In addition, the doctor prescribed a sedative that would make the pawnbroker sleep more soundly.

. . . DAY FOUR . . .

Father Bellini was up and out of the rectory early on the morning of Saturday, October 16th. In the fall of the year, Bellini's schedule called for him to referee the Saturday morning games of the CYO league on the football field behind Saint Alomar. As usual, there were three games scheduled, and it was part of Father Bellini's responsibility to see that the games were completed by noon.

When he left the rectory that morning, he advised Mrs. Heart, the housekeeper, that he would be at the CYO football field all morning, have lunch with his widowed mother in Massapequa around one o'clock, then stop by the Chambers house later that afternoon.

Mrs. Heart, as was her custom, dutifully made

note of Bellini's itinerary and put it on the bulletin board next to the Monsignor's schedule.

When Father Bellini left his mother's house in Massapequa, he told her he would call her on Sunday evening. Joseph Bellini never made that call—nor did he show up at the Chambers house. There were unconfirmed reports of him having been seen at the house on 112 Ocean Avenue late that afternoon, but there is no record of anyone having talked to him after he left Massapequa.

While Father Bellini officiated at the CYO games, Lester Chambers and Kooch Webster returned to the house at 112 Ocean Avenue. It was still raining, and the boys were soaked by the time they arrived at their destination. They went to the kennel behind the house where Kooch had stored the items he intended to take to Silverman's pawnshop. Kooch kicked open the wire gate around the kennel, opened the door and peered in.

"Hey, they're gone!"

Lester peered in over his friend's shoulder. "What's gone?"

"The stuff," Kooch fumed. "Some son-of-a-bitch took all our stuff."

Lester double-checked. "I'll bet somebody saw you puttin' it in there," he speculated.

Kooch studied the adjacent houses and conceded it was a possibility. "Hey, we just go in and get something else."

"Let's not," Lester said. "We're just gonna' get in more trouble if we do."

Lester's warning fell on deaf ears. Kooch was already on his way through the back door. Once inside, he stopped. The items he had carefully stored in the kennel were now neatly arranged in the hallway leading to the front of the house. "Hey, Lester, look at this."

Lester looked around his friend into the darkness. "It's a sign," he muttered. "We ain't supposed to go in there."

"Sign? What's that supposed to mean?" Kooch said. "What yer really sayin' is you're scared. Them things bein' moved ain't got nothin' to do with signs. Some asshole is just tryin' to play a trick on us."

"Look, Kooch, let's get out of here. I've had enough of this creepy place." The word "creepy" gave him away. He knew it the moment he said it.

"The only thing creepy about all this is the way you turn chicken every few minutes," Kooch chided. "The only way this coulda happened is if you told somebody. Did ya?"

"I ain't told nobody," he lied. Lester was prone to playing childish games with himself; Alice May wasn't a somebody—she was his stepmother.

Kooch was on the verge of another accusation when they heard footsteps on the porch. Before either of the boys could react, Roy Chambers had thrown the door open and was standing in the doorway glaring at them.

Justice, Roy Chambers style, was swift. The boys were herded into the car. Kooch was dropped off at his house, where Mr. Chambers told Charla Webster that the boys had been stealing. Then he drove home with his son. Lester was sent to his room and told to stay there until his father decided on the appropriate punishment. From his room, Lester could hear his father's angry shouts at his stepmother.

At 2:30, Roy Chambers opened the door to his son's room, instructed him to pull down his pants and bend over the edge of the bed. Then, either by chance or design, using the belt Lester had brought home from the former Lutz house, he proceeded to administer a beating with the buckle end of the belt. In her journal, Alice described standing at the bottom of the stairs leading to the second floor, listening to her husband's profane outrage. She carefully penned the words "bastard" and "whoreson" as part of that entry. "His rage spent," she wrote, "he instructed the eleven year-old to clean himself up and act like he had a halfway decent upbringing."

Kooch, on the other hand, defied his mother and grandmother when they attempted to reprimand him for his behavior. "You can't punish me for goin' in there," he challenged. "It's just an old dump that don't mean nothin' to nobody."

"Mr. Chambers said you and Lester have been stealing things from that house." With that single charge, Charla claimed to be at her wit's end with her son's behavior and turned the matter over to her mother, Jacalyn Cordes.

Mrs. Cordes went to the hall closet and took out the items her daughter had found in her grandson's room. "Where did these come from?" Even as mentally agile as she knew the boy was, she knew he would be hard pressed to come up with an acceptable explanation.

Kooch didn't even try. "So what? They don't belong to nobody. Lester told me that old place has been empty for years."

"The point is, they aren't yours, and when you take things that don't belong to you, that constitutes stealing."

At that point, Kooch apparently realized that his defiant approach wasn't working and resorted to a different tactic. Suddenly, in the heat of the argument, he hung his head, shuffled his feet and declared that he was sorry. At the same time, he promised the two women he would not go back to the house on Ocean Avenue.

This unexpected act of contrition by the normally rebellious Kooch triggered an immediate softening in the two women's approach. He was confined to the house for the rest of the day, but that was to be the extent of his punishment. Two days later, Kooch would tell Lester Chambers that he had put the stolen gold-encased Bulova watch in his grandmother's purse to get even with her. When Lester asked him why, Kooch said that if his grandmother should happen to be stopped by the police, they would suspect her of stealing it. Kooch did not explain why he thought the police would stop her in the first place.

Lester meanwhile watched television in sober silence with the rest of the family. On one occasion he left the room to get something from the refrigerator; when he did, he overheard his father thank Ellen for having the courage to tell him what the two boys were doing at the former Lutz house. Prior to that, Lester had been convinced that his stepmother was responsible for informing his father.

That evening, Lester confronted Ellen and threatened her.

"You better be careful," she cautioned him. "There's a lot more I haven't told him. He still doesn't know anything about you smoking pot. You keep threatening me, and I'll tell him about that, too."

The knock on the door at the Webster house came shortly after 6:00 P.M. Kooch was in the living room watching television, his mother and grandmother having gone to the supermarket. When he answered the door, he was surprised to see Moe Williams. The man was leaning against the doorjamb, his foot wedged in the door so that Kooch couldn't shut it. He was slapping a short, heavy metal club against the palm of his left hand.

"It's Saturday, piss ant. Where's my money?"

"I—I haven't got it yet," Kooch said nervously.

"Hey, you're out of time, sonny boy. When Moe says Saturday he means Saturday."

"I—I can get it tomorrow," Kooch bargained.

Moe shook his head, "Not tomorrow—now! I want it now."

Kooch had resorted to stealing money from the envelope his mother kept in her top dresser drawer before. She called it her emergency fund, and Kooch knew she usually kept anywhere from ten to twenty dollars in the hiding place. "Look," he pleaded, "give me a couple of minutes. I think I know where I can find some. Wait here."

Kooch raced upstairs to his mother's bedroom, rifled through the drawer until he found the envelope and opened it. He breathed a sigh of relief. There was a twenty dollar bill in it. He grabbed it, spun around and was looking straight into the pockmarked face of Moe Williams. "You better get out of here," he stammered. "My mom will hear you and come up here."

"Is that so?" Moe said, "Funny, I could have sworn I saw her and another old lady leave in a car twenty minutes ago. Maybe you ought to call her up here, huh?"

Kooch swallowed hard.

"Go on, sonny boy," Moe taunted, "call for Mama. Lets see what happens."

Kooch held out his hand with the twenty dollars in it. It was trembling.

73

"Ain't enough, sonny boy. When you don't pay Moe on time, Moe charges interest—one hundred percent interest. Now you owe Moe twenty-four dollars."

"But that's all I got," Kooch quaked.

Moe Williams reached out with one hand and grabbed the money. With the other he brought the heavy metal club up in an arc. It crushed into Kooch's groin and ricocheted into his crotch, catapulting the boy backward across the bedroom. Reeling, he tumbled backward over his mother's bed and landed on the floor, dazed, whimpering and vomiting.

"Next time, sonny boy, when you want Moe's services, you pay up front. Moe knows he can't trust you no more. Dig?"

Eyes stinging with tears, the taste of bile and stomach acids still swirling around in his mouth, Kooch nodded dumbly. He was doubled up with the pain where Moe had clubbed him and couldn't stand up.

Still grinning, Moe slipped the metal rod in his pocket and started to turn away, then paused. "I know what you're thinking, sonny boy. You're thinking you'll just get your stuff from somebody else. Well, I got news for you. It don't work that way, piss ant. Your skinny little ass belongs to me now."

It was 10:15 P.M. when Mrs. Heart knocked on the door of Monsignor McConnell's study in the Saint Alomar rectory. The Monsignor had instructed his housekeeper to see if she could locate Father Bellini. McConnell was not feeling well and wanted to warn the young priest that if his condition did not improve by morning, Bellini would have to substitute for him at the late Mass.

"What is it?" McConnell asked.

Mrs. Heart opened the door. Her face was uncommonly white, and she was wringing her hands.

"That . . . that was the police," Mrs. Heart stammered.

"What about the police?"

"T-t-they are on their way over. They found Father Bellini's car."

"What do you mean they found his car? Where is Joseph?"

"They don't know." Her voice was quaking.

McConnell felt his face flush. "You're speaking in riddles, Mrs. Heart. Who, pray tell, are they?"

"The police," she repeated.

McConnell's face, normally quite ruddy, drained of color and turned an ashen gray. He slumped backward with his hand over his heart. "Something has happened to Joseph?"

Mrs. Heart would later admit she did not know whether to stay with the Monsignor or answer the door when the bell rang. Only after McConnell assured her that he would be all right did she finally answer it.

Within minutes, Mrs. Heart returned and

ushered a tall, intense man into McConnell's study. The man was holding out a police badge. "My name is Lt. Jerome Steinberg," he said. "Police—homicide."

McConnell sat upright, staring up at the man.

"Sorry to bother you at this hour, sir, but we found Father Bellini's car down on Ocean Avenue. It was parked in the driveway of the old Lutz place. Someone in the neighborhood reported that the car had been sitting there since early afternoon and they thought something might be wrong. Deputy Sherman of the county sheriff's department checked it out and called us in."

"But . . . but you said 'homicide,'" McConnell stammered.

"That's right, sir. At this point we don't know anything for certain, because we haven't been able to locate Father Bellini. Have you heard from him?"

McConnell shook his head. "But why homicide, Lieutenant?"

"Because we found this. Could this be Father Bellini's?" Steinberg was holding a Roman collar, streaked with blood.

McConnell took it and examined the way the button in the back appeared to have been ripped out. "Good grief, Lieutenant, do you think Joseph has come to harm?"

"We don't know, Monsignor. That's why we're here."

"You say you found Father Bellini's car at the old Lutz place?" McConnell asked.

THE NIGHTMARE CONTINUES

Steinberg nodded. "Yes, sir. Are you familiar with it?"

McConnell sagged wearily back in his chair with his eyes closed. "Oh, God," he moaned, "not again."

... DAY FIVE ...

It was the custom for Saint Alomar students to sit with their class at Mass on Sunday morning. Because of this, Lester noted that Kooch wasn't present. Concerned that his friend had gotten into more trouble than he was willing to admit, Lester called Kooch when he returned home from church. Jacalyn Cordes answered the phone. When she realized that Lester was the boy her grandson was with when he was caught stealing, her voice turned icy.

"Donald is sick. He can't come to the phone. And—I don't think I want him talking to someone like you anyway." Before Lester could say anything, the woman hung up.

Unable to bridge the gap with his father following his punishment, Lester discussed the call with the only other available person—his stepmother. Alice later recorded in her journal that she felt sorry for the boy and prayed for the wisdom to explain Jacalyn Cordes behavior.

As it turned out, it would be several days before Lester learned about the Moe Williams incident. At first, the limping Kooch lied about the large discolored area around his groin. He told Lester he had fallen down the back steps while carrying out the trash. Only after seeing the extent of the bruise in gym class did Lester learn the truth.

In the Webster house, Charla and her mother spent much of the long, dreary afternoon unpacking boxes still unopened from the family's recent move. Kooch remained in his room throughout the day, telling his mother and grandmother he felt sick to his stomach. While the women went about the tedious chore, they talked about their plans to spend Christmas in Florida with Mrs. Cordes' older sister. For the first time in weeks, Jacalyn Cordes told her sister, Charla appeared to be on top of the situation.

Jerome Steinberg, himself recently divorced and living in a small condominium south of Copiaqua overlooking Oyster Bay, had nothing better to do so he went to his office at the Suffolk County police department. The Bellini disappearance was still very much on his mind.

Steinberg was a rookie policeman on the night of November 13, 1974, when Ronald

DeFio drugged his family at dinner and then shot them with a high-powered rifle. He had been assigned other duties during the events that followed, but he was intimately familiar, as was everyone in the department, with the DeFio case.

When he stepped out of his cruiser the previous evening to check Bellini's car, the DeFio murders and the subsequent bizarre sequence of events endured by the Lutz family came back to him.

Steinberg would remember that he greeted the dispatcher, poured himself a cup of coffee and inquired if there had been any word on Bellini. Told that there were no new developments, he went into his cubicle and sat down at his desk. The first thing he noticed was a brown paper sack full of textbooks. A note was attached. "Jerry, got busy and forgot what you told me to do with these."

Steinberg admitted that he himself had forgotten all about Sara Wine's request.

He picked up the sack, spilled the contents out on his desk, opened them and remembered that they were to be returned to Saint Alomar. Only then did he recall the sum and substance of his conversation with the local truant officer. The books were left behind by some kids playing around the old Lutz house. The books, according to the note inside the flyleaf, were from the Saint Alomar book leasing program. He had two names: Lester Chambers and Donald Webster. Did that somehow tie in to the fact that the missing Father Bellini was from Saint Alomar? And was it anything other than coincidence that Bellini's car was found at 112 Ocean Avenue?

Curiously, Steinberg mused, he hadn't thought about the old Lutz place in years. Now it had come up twice in the last 48 hours.

He made a terse note on his desk pad. "Check on these kids first thing Monday morning."

In the village of Westover, some 70 miles from Amityville, Gloria Peranson walked out of her recreation room to answer the telephone. As far as she was concerned, the caller was calling at a very inconvenient time. Gloria and her husband, Abe, were watching a subscription concert of the New York Philharmonic on pay television.

"Hello," she said abruptly, making no attempt to mask the irritation in her voice. She was hoping the caller would take note of her tone and realize they were interrupting something.

"Gloria," the distressed voice asked, "is that you?" Even with the unfamiliar raspy quality of the voice, she recognized it as her father, Leon Silverman.

"Daddy? Is that you? What's the matter?"

"I . . . I need help."

"What's the matter?" she repeated. Abe Peranson would later describe his wife's voice as instantly hysterical.

"It . . . it's . . . after me."

"What's after you?" Gloria screamed.

During one of the many interrogations that followed, Gloria Peranson would tell police that she was convinced her father had said "that thing—that thing—that thing." She would also admit that she herself was in a state of panic. She could only say what she thought she had heard, and she admitted that she could be mistaken.

It was during the course of her third police interview and her first with Lt. Jerome Steinberg that, in attempting to describe what she heard in the background that night, she used the words "whirling" and "grinding noise."

. . . DAY SIX . . .

The phone rang in Jerome Steinberg's Copiaqua condominium at 3:43 A.M. The call was from the Suffolk County police department night dispatcher. "Up and at 'em, Jerry baby. Carr needs you."

Steinberg, rubbing sleep-heavy eyes, asked where.

"3131 Sixth Street, behind Silverman's Pawnshop in Amityville. From what Carr tells me this one is right up your alley."

"Homicide?"

"I don't think there's much doubt about it, but that's for you to decide."

Steinberg hung up the phone remembering that his former wife, Jill, hated these middle-of-the-night calls even more than he did. He dressed, brushed his teeth and slipped his electric razor in his coat pocket. Steinberg prided himself on the fact that he was in the car and pulling out of the condo parking lot less than five minutes after getting the call.

Fifteen minutes later he was walking through the rear entrance to 3131 Sixth Street. An officer was standing in the kitchen trying to console a middle-aged couple. The woman was crying; the man merely looked befuddled.

"Carr is upstairs," the officer said.

At the top of the stairs, he saw Stephen Carr, the Chief of the Suffolk County Police Department. "In here, Jerry," Carr called.

Steinberg described the following scene to John Kelly. There is little doubt that John tape-recorded that conversation and then transcribed it for his files, word for word.

"In the last few years it's gotten a little hairier out here on the island. We seem to have more sickos than we use to, and consequently we have more homicides. A couple of years ago, the backlog of cases got so heavy that Steve Carr had to step in and help me. He was the first one called out to Silverman's place that night because he was the one on duty that weekend. Carr is a real pro—a lot better at investigating than he is at administration. When I walked in that room I knew everything was still just the way he found it. Stephen is the kind of guy who wouldn't touch anything if he intended to ask my opinion about things.

"The victim was an elderly white male. He

was dressed in pajamas and had his teeth out. There was a phone lying at his feet. It wasn't until my second conversation with Gloria Peranson three days later that I put two and two together and figured out the old man was on the phone to her when he was attacked. She was too hysterical to make much sense that first night.

"I guess there's no other way to say it—he was screwed right into the wall next to his bed. His assailant used an antique wood auger. Drove the damn thing right through his heart and into the wall behind him—and just left him hanging there. Whoever did it was strong as an ox. The old man was too fat for the auger to go all the way through him and into the wall so the killer had to crush Silverman's chest first. Maybe a better description would be flattened or smashed.

"To this day I haven't been able to figure out how the killer did it. Carr is extremely thorough. He had the place gone over from top to bottom but found nothing—nowhere—not even in those places a killer usually slips up."

The Suffolk County deputy coroner was also there along with the patrolman that had assisted Abe and Gloria Peranson in getting into the locked house. At 4:55 the body was removed, and Carr and Steinberg spent the next hour talking to Abe Peranson. At 5:30, the two officers sat in Steinberg's car reviewing what they had.

"Helluva way to start the new week," Carr observed.

Steinberg busied himself going over what he

had already learned. "Doors were locked, windows ditto—all from the inside. The Doc says Silverman had been dead for several hours by the time they got into the house."

"Don't forget the cat," Carr reminded him.

"Yeah, how about that? What kind of sicko takes time to stop and kill the cat, too?"

While Steinberg went over his notes, Carr lit up a cigarette. The two men parceled out what they knew had to be done in the next few hours with Carr taking the bulk of responsibility for the investigation because of Steinberg's involvement with the Bellini matter.

"I can put our missing priest on the back burner for a couple of days," he offered.

Carr shook his head. "No, I'll stay on top of this. Do what you can with the Bellini case and keep checking with me. I got a hunch I'm going to have my hands full when our friends in the media get their hooks in this one."

Shortly after Lester and Ellen Chambers left for school that Monday morning, Alice Chambers called Dr. Leonard Crispman, the family doctor. Alice was concerned about the persistent, growing black stain on her stepson's hand. Sister Alfonsa's treatment, even though she was a nurse, had failed to curb its spread. Asked repeatedly by both his father and stepmother, Lester maintained that there was no discomfort associated with his growing affliction. (There is some evidence however that Lester complained of a persistent itching sensation to Donald Webster. It may have been that he was reluctant to talk to anyone besides Kooch about it because he would have to reveal to someone other than his stepmother how the stain came about.)

The entry in Mrs. Chambers' journal for the previous day indicated that Sunday, October 17th, had passed without event. After Mass and Lester's call to the Webster boy, Lester watched an NFL game in the afternoon while Roy Chambers read. Late in the afternoon, the family went for a drive out on the island. Because of the deteriorating weather, the outing was cut short, and they returned home in time for Ellen to attend a youth group meeting at Saint Agnes. Since Alice always recorded the things she discussed with her husband, it is safe to assume that she said nothing about the footnote in Bishop Jacquess' book. It may well have been because she did not want to alarm her husband prematurely.

Alice was still on the telephone when the doorbell rang. When she answered the door, she was confronted by a tall, somewhat dissheveled man with bushy black hair and similar eyebrows. She noted in her diary that the man had "intensely dark and probing eyes" and that he needed a shave.

"Good morning, Mrs. Chambers. I am Lt. Jerome Steinberg of the Suffolk County Police Department. Sorry to bother you like this, but I have a few questions I would like to ask you. May I come in?"

For obvious reasons, Alice assumed that the

officer was there to talk about Lester's involvement with the stolen articles from the house on Ocean Avenue. Her opening question after seating him in the living room betrayed her apprehension.

"Is this about Lester?"

"Well—yes and no. Actually I'm here about Father Bellini over at Saint Alomar. We can talk about your son later."

Alice was both relieved and puzzled.

"I understand Father Bellini stopped by to see you Saturday afternoon at your request. Do you recall what time he left here?"

"On the contrary, Lieutenant, Father Bellini didn't show up. I waited for him all afternoon."

Steinberg extracted a small spiral notebook and began to take notes. "Was Father Bellini coming to see you about the matter you discussed with him at the rectory on Friday?"

The way Steinberg phrased the question, Alice assumed that he already knew about Lester and Donald Webster. She immediately launched into a long and detailed description of the occurrences that led up to her asking Father Bellini for help.

"Did your son tell you where he intended to fence the items he stole?"

"Fence?"

"Pawn—sell," Steinberg explained.

"At Mr. Silverman's shop on High Street."

Steinberg made notes throughout the course of their conversation. These same notes were the ones he referred to repeatedly during his two taping sessions with John Kelly.

"At church yesterday," Alice began cautiously, "there was talk that Father Bellini had disappeared. Is there any truth to that?"

"We haven't been able to locate him," Steinberg said, being equally cautious. "We received a report that Father Bellini was seen at the same house where your son and his friend admitted stealing things."

"Was he all right?"

"Well, actually no one saw him. They saw his car. After it sat there for several hours, the neighbors reported it to the police department."

Despite her penchant for detail throughout her diary, Alice recorded that she recalled very little of her conversation with the officer from that point on. She did write the following:

> *"After hearing the news of Father Bellini's disappearance, I felt a strange sadness. More than that, I had an overwhelming feeling of foreboding. As was the case with Lester's jacket, I sensed the presence of evil."*

Steinberg handed over Lester's textbooks and drove directly to 112 Ocean Avenue. His investigation was cursory, but he did check the kennel where Mrs. Chambers indicated the two boys claimed they had stored the items overnight. When he tried the rear door to the house, it was locked. He recorded all of this in his notebook along with another notation: "Court order—112 O.A." He would say that the latter referred to the fact that he needed a court order to reopen the house because of legalities relating to a crime scene.

After leaving the Lutz house, Steinberg stopped at a convenience store on Parker Street and then drove to the Webster house. He spoke briefly with Jacalyn Cordes who informed him that her daughter was out of town. Steinberg later verified that Charla Webster was in Boston on business and was not scheduled to return until later in the week.

From the Webster house he drove to Saint Alomar and inquired about the availability of Monsignor McConnell. He wanted to update the priest on his progress in the Bellini matter.

In the Saint Alomar rectory, Mrs. Heart informed him that the Monsignor was grief-stricken over Bellini's disappearance. "Monsignor has been conducting a prayer vigil and fasting in the hope that his small sacrifice will help," Mrs. Heart said.

Steinberg was escorted to McConnell's second floor study and shown into a darkened room where the only illumination was a single candle.

"Sorry to bother you again, sir—" Steinberg cut his greeting short, however, when he saw the effects of the sleepless vigil on the old man. His face was drawn and lined. In the flickering light of the candle, McConnell looked almost ghostly. McConnell had remained on his knees, praying and fasting since Saturday night. The Monsignor seemed so weak that Steinberg decided not to discuss the Bellini matter with him and left.

It was almost five o'clock when Steinberg pulled into the parking lot of the Suffolk County police station. He went into Carr's office and dropped wearily into the chair across from the chief. "Any word on Bellini?"

Carr shook his head.

"What about the Silverman case?"

Carr rocked back in his chair and folded his hands behind his head. "Watch the news tonight. You'll get the flavor."

"Rough day?"

Carr smiled. "Jerry, my friend, before this one is over, we're going to have a goddamn circus on our hands. It's already started."

Roy Chambers got up from the dinner table and went into the living room to turn on the television. He did not watch television for entertainment. The local cable television company carried a 24-hour news service which was the only thing he watched. There was a flurry of commercials, and a somewhat officious voice announced that he was watching WCNA's headline news.

"Suffolk County Police continue to investigate the bizarre death of Amityville pawnshop owner Leon Silverman. Silverman's brutally slain body was found in his second floor bedroom early Monday morning by his daughter. Silverman had been murdered with an antique wood auger."

While the gray-haired reader droned on in melodramatic tones, the television screen displayed scenes of both the interior and exterior of Silverman's home. There was also a brief shot of the discreetly covered body being carried to the ambulance. The camera then panned to a young woman reporter standing in front of Silverman's house.

"Mrs. Paranson, Silverman's daughter, told police she received a frantic phone call from her father late Sunday evening. Her father, she told us, was hysterical and indicated that he was in danger of being attacked. Mrs. Peranson then drove to her father's home, found the house dark and the door locked, contacted Suffolk County police and requested their assistance.

"The police were with Mrs. Peranson when she discovered her father's body. Police Chief Stephen Carr tells us that the assailant used an antique wood auger to murder his victim . . ."

Alice Chambers had followed her husband into the living room and watched in horror as the story unfolded. The moment Silverman's name was mentioned, she connected it to Lester's admission that they had pawned their items at Silverman's shop.

She did not wait for the end of the telecast but hastened to Lester's room where she knew the boy was studying. "Do you remember what you told me you and Donald took to Mr. Silverman?" she asked.

Lester nodded.

"Tell me again," she insisted.

"I—I took a dish, an old one, and Kooch hocked some old tool. He called it a wood angle or somethin' like that."

Alice Chambers wrote in her journal that she felt "icy fingers crawl up her back" when her stepson confirmed that Donald Webster had been the one that pawned what was in all probability the death instrument.

In his condo, Jerome Steinberg was seated at the kitchen table. Spread out in front of him were such items as his day log, the investigating report on Bellini's car, a crime scene analysis of the Silverman murder, several odds and ends of paper and a map.

For reasons he could not yet explain, he was developing a gut feeling about the convoluted series of events. In a subsequent conversation with John Kelly, he revealed that at that point he had not tied the wood auger used in the Silverman killing to the theft from the house at 112 Ocean Avenue.

AUTHOR'S NOTE: STRANGELY OMITTED FROM JOHN KELLY'S OTHERWISE COMPREHENSIVELY DOCUMENTED FILE ON THIS INCIDENT IS THE BACKGROUND OF JEROME STEINBERG PRIOR TO JOINING THE SUFFOLK COUNTY POLICE DEPARTMENT.

STEINBERG SERVED IN THE MILITARY PRIOR TO BEGINNING HIS POLICE CAREER. AN OFFICER IN THE UNITED STATES ARMY, HIS PRIMARY ASSIGNMENT WAS WITH THE

OFFICE OF THE ADJUTANT GENERAL AS A SPECIAL INVESTIGATOR. STEINBERG FREQUENTLY CREDITED HIS UNCANNY ABILITY TO RECALL THE PRECISE SEQUENCE OF EVENTS TO HIS MILITARY TRAINING.

The evening of Monday, October 18th, Jerome Steinberg meticulously retraced his day. He constructed a convoluted diagram that included the meandering odyssey of Father Joseph Bellini from the rectory to the CYO football fields to his mother's house in Massapequa and finally to the address on Ocean Avenue. Then he overlaid that with what he knew about the two boys who had stolen articles from the same house. Finally, he introduced the bizarre murder of Leon Silverman to his collage.

As yet there was no solution to his puzzle. For the moment all he had was more questions.

He studied the diagram for several minutes and then decided to call it a day.

. . . DAY SEVEN . . .

Tuesday, October 19th, dawned cold and gray. At the Chambers house, Ellen left for school and Roy for work, but Lester stayed home. Alice had scheduled a midmorning appointment with Dr. Crispman.

In the Webster household, Mrs. Cordes put her grandson on the bus and tried to place a call to her daughter in Boston. The story of the brutal attack on Leon Silverman was still front page news two days after his death. As Jacalyn Cordes dialed her daughter's hotel number, she held a copy of the morning paper in her hand. The headlines indicated that there had been no new developments in the case. Under the headlines were two pictures. One was of the room where Silverman's body was found; the other was a picture of Silverman's cat, Tramaine, lying beside an empty china bowl.

Lester would not see these pictures until later in the day. When Kooch saw it, he immediately recognized the bowl as the one Lester had pawned. The illustration of the chained cross showed through clearly even in the newsprint quality of the picture.

At Saint Alomar, Monsignor McConnell was beginning his third day of fasting. Mrs. Heart meanwhile carefully combed the pages of the newspapers and waited expectantly by the phone for news of Father Bellini.

Jerome Steinberg started his day with a quick breakfast and a telephone call to Stephen Carr to start the process of getting a court order that would permit him to conduct an investigation of the house on Ocean Avenue. His schedule indicated that he had another full day ahead of him.

Alice Chambers waited for Lester to finish putting on his shirt and step into the outer office. Dr. Crispman stepped out of the room, washed his hands and returned. He waited until the door closed behind the boy, then he sat down at his desk and leaned forward.

"I can't be certain, Alice, but I don't like what I see."

The woman braced herself. In the short period of time she had been married to Roy Chambers, she had now been to Crispman's office no less than four times—once with Ellen, twice for herself. Crispman was the straightforward type who did not mince words.

"This is a little out of my line, Alice, but I believe I've run across this once before. That was several years ago, but it looks like the same thing—and it smells like it. I'm certain you noticed it has a very characteristic odor."

Alice had noticed the peculiar odor which smelled something like burnt almonds to her.

"I think we've got a rare form of something that's turning out to be quite common these days—lentigo maligna melanoma, a form of skin cancer."

Alice leaned forward, alarmed. "Cancer?"

"Remember, I said I'm not at all certain. That's why I'm going to send you and Lester to see a colleague of mine."

"But if it is skin cancer . . ." she started to ask.

Crispman held up his hand. "We won't even talk about it until we know for certain. In the meantime, though, I want you to guard Lester against hurting himself—cuts, bruises, that sort of thing. If he's in any kind of sports activity I think you should hold him out until we get a handle on this."

The doctor opened his desk drawer, took out a notebook and began to rifle through the pages until he came to the name he was looking for.

"I want you to take Lester to see a man by the name of Lawrence Spielmann. This should be right down his alley. He'll know whether or not

I'm on target the moment he sees Lester." He scratched out Spielmann's name and phone number on a piece of paper and handed it to her. "When you get home, call him and make an appointment. In the meantime, I'll have contacted Larry and have it all set up for you."

"Is there anything I can do for Lester until Dr. Spielmann can see him?"

"If you're asking me if there is anything you can put on it to slow it, the answer is no. If my diagnosis is right, the intervention for malignant melanoma is predicated solely on the histopathologic level of the invasion. There are several ways to get after it, Alice, if it is in fact cancer. There is always surgery, but someone like Spielmann might suggest chemotherapy or immunotherapy. I don't think he would recommend radiation for a boy Lester's age. But this kind of talk is getting the cart before the horse. Let's see what Dr. Spielmann thinks."

When Alice stood up, her knees were shaking. The doctor walked around the desk and took her hand. "You can help matters by keeping your chin up," he advised her. "A couple of months ago, Roy was the one who needed you. Now it's Lester."

"What should I tell Lester?"

"If he were my son, I'd tell him we don't know yet. Just tell him we'll have to do more tests. A boy Lester's age has enough to worry about without causing him undue alarm."

Outside, greeted by a blustery wind, Lester

looked at the woman who had replaced his mother. "What did he say? Is it serious?"

Alice bit her lip. "We just don't know yet."

Jerome Steinberg sat across the room from the two men and waited for a response. Neither of them seemed inclined to volunteer an answer. "Would you like me to repeat the question?"

"The problem, Lieutenant, is that neither Father Chiraldi nor I know quite how to answer your question. Neither of us were here during the DeFio tragedy, nor were we here when the Lutz family went through their ordeal. And while it's true that the owner of the house did seek assistance from this office, the situation was resolved before the church intervened."

"According to our records, all you recommended was that he seek the aid of some institution down in the Carolinas. Is that correct?"

"You must understand, Lieutenant, in the perspective of the Holy Mother Church, there are five things to be considered when we investigate situations that seem to indicate some sort of diabolical involvement. First, Lieutenant, we must ask ourselves—is there any possibility of fraud or deception? After we've passed that hurdle we must determine if the phenomena is the result of natural or scientific causes. After that we must eliminate any possibility that we might be dealing with something in the realm of the parapsychological world. If we get that far, we deal with the question of influences by forces from the diabolical realm."

"You said there were five," Steinberg reminded him.

"Last, but by no means least, Lieutenant, we consider the rarest occurrence of all—a miracle. Few of us, however, are ever privileged to experience one."

"What you're telling me is that it's going to take some time," Steinberg said.

"You're the one who is raising the question, Lieutenant. You tell us, what do you think we're dealing with?"

"Gentlemen, I don't know. It's that plain and that simple." There was a note of exasperation in Steinberg's voice. "I am not familiar with your doctrine, your procedures and methodologies, or your way of looking at things like haunted houses, ghosts and things that go around hurting people."

"Are you telling us you believe the house is haunted?" Father Cannon asked. He was the older of the two priests and had the pugnacious manner of a man accustomed to standing up for the church's often unpopular views.

"I don't know what I believe, Father Cannon, but I think I need some help in determining just what the hell is going on over there."

Chiraldi leaned forward. "There are all kinds of things to consider, Lieutenant. As a parapsychologist, I can tell you that we view the field as being divided into two arenas—ESP and psychokinesis. When we are dealing with ESP, there are a number of things to consider—mental telepathy, clairvoyance and precognition. Psychokinesis is an altogether different matter. During the Lutz episode, Father Nuncio believed that there were psychokinetic influences at work."

"Father Nuncio?" Steinberg repeated.

"That's right. The church's involvement at that time went no higher up than Father Nuncio, a simple parish priest."

"What you're really telling me is that the church did not come to any official conclusion?"

"In a nutshell, Lieutenant, that is correct. Father Nuncio made a recommendation, and there is nothing in our files to indicate whether the parties involved at that time followed up on it or not."

"So, where does that leave us?"

"I'm afraid that leaves us right back at the beginning, Lieutenant," Chiraldi said. "On the other hand, I do have an idea. I know someone who may be able to shed some light on this. Let me discuss this matter with them. If they think they can be of some assistance to you, I'll get back in touch with you. Just leave me a number where you can be reached."

Steinberg handed Chiraldi his card, thanked the two priests for their time and drove to the Suffolk County police department.

The dining room of the Saint Alomar Academy was divided by a large floor-to-ceiling accordion-type folding wall. Boys ate on one side, girls on the other.

The boys wore white shirts, blue pants and blue ties, and on Friday they endured the added humiliation of a blue blazer with the Saint Alomar crest emblazoned on the pocket.

The girls did not fare much better. They were saddled with a mundane ensemble consisting of white blouses, blue skirts, white socks and brown penny loafers. The colder months afforded them the opportunity to don blue sweaters, but the color options ended with navy blue.

None of this mattered to Lester, who gave even less thought to the dress code than he did his studies. In fact, Lester's only real complaint was the decidedly preferential treatment his sister, Ellen, received by attending Saint Agnes Girl's School. It was Ellen's bonus, his father repeatedly reminded him, for testing out as a gifted student.

The fact that his 13-year-old sister always brought home better grades than he did was no longer a source of irritation to Lester. He consoled himself with his achievements in a male fantasy world by volunteering to open jars and garage doors, mowing the lawn and occasionally fixing things around the house.

On his way into the Saint Alomar cafeteria, he encountered Kooch.

"What did the doctor say? Did he tell you ya got the creeping crud?"

"Naaa—all he said was I gotta' see another doctor."

Kooch had been hoping for something a bit more dramatic, but going to see another doctor wasn't all that dramatic.

By the time they were seated, Kooch had changed the subject. "Hey, did ya see the pictures in the paper?"

"Pictures of what?"

"Of old man Silverman's place—the place where he died."

"Old man Silverman is dead?" Lester asked.

"Yeah, somebody killed him—and they used that wood auger I pawned."

Lester stopped with his sandwich halfway to his mouth. "Awww, you're jerkin' my chain. Nobody killed Silverman."

"Did, too. It's right there on the front page of the paper. They even got a picture of that dumb cat of his. The killer croaked it, too. There's a picture of your bowl, too."

Lester stopped eating altogether. He turned and looked at Kooch with a look of disbelief on his face.

"Come on, jerk off, if you don't believe me, go into the school library and ask to see the morning paper. Then you'll see."

Lester did just that. Sister Karen, the librarian, would tell John Kelly it was the only time she ever saw Lester Chambers in the Saint Alomar school library.

That evening, during Lester's new, rigidly enforced study period after dinner, Ellen slipped into his room. "Hey, I thought we had a deal," she reminded him.

The girl had interrupted her brother in the middle of a daydream, and he gave her a perplexed look.

"Where's the stuff you promised?"

"I haven't been back there," Lester lied.

"Have too," Ellen taunted. "I know all about it."

"Alice told ya?"

"'Course not, you dummy. Prissy old Alice don't have to tell me anything. If I want to know something, all I have to do is slip into her and Dad's room and read her dumb old journal. Everytime you go whining to her and spill your guts, she writes it down in her journal. It makes very interesting reading."

Lester felt his stomach do a slow roll. No wonder he was in trouble all the time. He thought he could trust his stepmother. Now he knew she was heading straight to his father with everything he told her. "She tricked me," he moaned, "I thought I could trust her."

There was something in the psychological makeup of Ellen that would not allow her to let someone else take the credit for anything— especially something as personally rewarding as her brother's misery. "Alice isn't your problem, dumbo. I am."

Lester leaped out of his chair and slammed his sister back against the wall.

"Hey, baby brother," she hissed, "don't use that muscle routine on me. I still got that little pot-smoking episode hanging over your head, remember?"

"I ain't been back to that house I tell ya."

"Maybe—maybe not," Ellen said, "but you can't prove it. It's my word against yours, and right now your name is mud around here."

Lester backed away. She had him. He knew he would have to think of something. He had a sick feeling in the pit of his stomach. "So what do you want?" he mumbled.

"I want what you promised."

"You want me to go back in that house after the beating Dad gave me?"

"You're the one that made the promise. Besides, how is Roy going to know if you don't tell Alice?"

Lester sagged down on the edge of his bed and looked at his stained hand. The blotch had started to creep up his wrist. More than anything else he wanted to stay away from that old house. But if there was something worse than going back in the house, it was his father learning about the pot-smoking incident. He looked up at his sister still shaking his head.

"Hey, it's up to you," she sneered, "but let me give you a piece of advice. Don't think about it too long, or it will be too late."

Jacalyn Cordes sat at the Albany Street railroad crossing waiting for the train to pass. The red and yellow warning lights on the crossing barrier blinked on and off, creating a hypnotic pattern of technicolor images in the interior of her BMW.

Impatient with the delay, she reached across the seat and pulled her purse toward her. Unzipping it with her right hand and keeping her left hand on the wheel, she opened it and began to grope in the darkness for the lambskin pouch that contained her cigarettes and lighter. Instead, her hand emerged with a tarnished gold Bulova watch. She could not recall having seen the watch before and wondered how it had gotten in her purse. Even more perplexing was the way it felt—very cold.

When the train cleared the crossing and the safety gates failed to lift, she put her car in reverse, backed up and pulled around the barrier—directly into the path of another oncoming train.

Do we assume that Jacalyn Cordes was still preoccupied with thoughts of the watch? Under oath, both the engineer and brakeman testified that they repeatedly sounded the approaching diesel's warning whistle.

The records of the Suffolk County police department list the time of the accident at 10:00 P.M., Tuesday, October 19. Print-outs from the traffic computer of the railroad indicate that the train passed the Albany intersection at precisely 9:57 P.M.

Some ten miles from the scene of the accident, at Republic Airport on Highway 110 east of Farmingdale, the WBAN entry made by the local weather observer indicates that the weather was clear with light and variable surface winds and unlimited visibility.

Two days later, Lt. Jerome Steinberg would stop by the Suffolk County coroner's office to pick up a copy of the autopsy report. The cause of death was listed as a heart attack prior to massive internal injury.

Clipped to the top of the report, however, was this note:

> *Richard:*
> *See note at bottom of page 2. Time of death was probably 9:57. It isn't often we get a victim wearing two watches to verify the time of death.*

The note was signed by Curtis Macklimore, the auxilary coroner at the time.

AUTHOR'S NOTE: THE FOLLOWING IS THE TEXT OF A NOTE CONTAINED IN JOHN KELLY'S FILE. IT WAS, AS ARE MOST OF JOHN'S NOTES, PRINTED IN METICULOUS BLOCK LETTERS. I HAVE INCLUDED IT AT THE CLOSE OF THIS SECTION BECAUSE I BELIEVE THE READER WILL FIND IT FASCINATING.

"The fact that both watches stopped at precisely 9:57 intrigued me. I was aware that her grandson, Donald, had put one of them in her purse, but knowing that the older one did

not work when he did so, the similarity in time is curious.

"I prevailed on Charla Webster to go through her mother's personal effects and retrieve the two watches.

"Several years earlier, my own father died of a heart attack. His watch stopped at the time of his death. Believing that I would like to wear the watch as a remembrance of him, I took it to be repaired. The jeweler told me that it was frozen up, indicating that someone had either held a magnet to it or was wearing it when they had a heart attack. He explained that watches being worn by a person during a heart attack often show evidence of some sort of massive magnetic action that occurs in the body during the attack.

"When I asked him to estimate the age of the two watches, he told me that the Lady Elpri was a fairly recent model. The Bulova, however, was estimated to be as much as forty-five years old. 'I doubt if that old Bulova has beat a tick in the last forty years,' he said.

"Still, I cannot ignore the fact that both watches stopped at precisely the same time."

FROM THE TEXT OF JOHN'S NOTE, WE CAN ONLY SPECULATE ABOUT HIS FASCINATION WITH MRS. CORDES' WATCHES. BUT I MUST ADMIT THAT I, TOO, FIND THIS INTRIGUING. WAS IT A ONE IN A MILLION COINCIDENCE, OR WAS IT SOME OTHER INFLUENCE?

. . . DAY EIGHT . . .

Stephen Carr of the Suffolk County police department was a soft-spoken, middle-aged man. A 20-year veteran of the force, he was the father of four sons and readily confessed to only one passion in life outside of his family and job—a fanatical allegiance to the New York Giants. A long-time officer in the police union, he was known for his investigative rather than administrative prowess.

Beside him in the car on this Wednesday morning was Jerome Steinberg, grim-faced, jaw set, apprehensive and staring through the rain-spattered windshield in stony silence. Steinberg had been up since four o'clock when a fellow officer called him after learning of the Cordes woman's oblique connection with the Bellini case.

Half an hour earlier, Carr had obtained the court order which permitted the two officers to conduct a search of the house at 112 Ocean Avenue.

Carr, aware that the usually affable Steinberg was preoccupied, had his own problems with the Silverman case. So far, he had made no real progress. Tying the murder weapon to the old house could hardly be considered a breakthrough.

He turned on to Ocean Avenue, mentally reviewing the tangled fragments and threads of information Steinberg had turned up over the past few days. Collectively they agreed that there were more than enough unanswered questions to justify the court order and the subsequent search of the house. Carr, fearing any kind of delay, had not told the issuing judge that one of his men had already conducted a cursory search the night Father Bellini's car was found in the driveway. He had given Steinberg a copy of the report and was not surprised when his long-time colleague rejected the officer's report as "far too sketchy for our purposes." Carr had to agree.

"How about it, Jerry? You've never committed yourself one way or the other." Carr laughed. "What do you think we're dealing with here?"

Steinberg scowled. The priests at the chancery had asked him the same question. "I guess I don't know what I think," he admitted. "I've never seen a ghost or a poltergeist." Steinberg would later tell John Kelly that he felt foolish even saying the word "ghost" aloud.

"You don't see poltergeists; you see what they do. You know—pictures falling off walls, things flying around the room, furniture moving. Ghosts are different. They don't throw stuff; they just hang around and try to scare the shit out of you."

"How do you know so much about this kind of thing?"

"I was involved the last time, remember? I did a lot of reading. Some of my questions still don't have answers."

Steinberg finally looked away from the window. "Okay, so tell me, what is going on in there—ghosts or poltergeists?"

Carr hesitated. "Want the official version or my version?"

"I've already read the official version. I took the files home last night. I want to know what you think."

"Off the record?"

"Off the record," Steinberg agreed.

Carr slumped in the seat as he drove. "Assuming you've got all your facts straight, whatever is going on in that old house is a helluva lot different this time than it was last time. When I talked to the couple that owned that house ten years ago, somebody or something was trying to scare the hell out of them. The bottom line is—pocketbooks got dented, but nobody got seriously hurt. That isn't the case this time, assuming your theory is right. You claim Silverman was involved, and he's been murdered. You tell me Bellini had his fingers in this thing, and now he's come up missing. Then, the first thing you tell me this morning is that the Cordes woman killed in that accident over near Glencoe last night is the grandmother of one of the boys involved in your investigation."

"None of which is conclusive about anything," Steinberg reminded him.

Carr nodded. "Right. So I figure you've either got the damndest string of coincidences going or—"

Steinberg was staring out the window again. "Or I've got nothing."

They arrived at 112 Ocean Avenue at precisely 10:00 A.M., according to the notation in Steinberg's day log, parked in the driveway and got out of the car.

"Wish I had a C-note for every time I've been in this old dump," Carr grunted. "For a while there, every parapsychological group in the eastern half of the country wanted to check it out. I've had 'em all—psychics, mediums, quacks, you name it. Even a TV producer that was thinking about doing a documentary on the place. Most of 'em only stayed a couple of hours, but one screwball stayed all night with infrared cameras, the whole nine yards."

"Did they learn anything?"

"If they did, they didn't tell me. It's like everything else; the minute the furor died down, so did the interest."

Steinberg lit up his first cigarette of the day, a monumental achievement since he had been up six hours at that point. He made a mental note to reward himself with a drink after work in acknowledgement of the accomplishment.

"Okay, so where do we start?" Carr asked.

"According to the one boy's stepmother, the boys got in initially by kicking out a basement window. Then they removed the stolen items through the back door and stored them in the kennel. On the other hand, when I was out here the other day, the back door was locked.

Carr nodded, looked up and assessed the heavy gray overcast. The early part of the morning had been clear and invigorating, but the weather had been deteriorating steadily. Now there was a raw wind off the ocean with a steady drizzle, and the temperature had fallen several degrees.

The two men walked along the side of the house, noted the broken basement window casing and climbed the steps to the back porch. From the porch they could see the empty swimming pool, the kennel and the boathouse.

"Suppose we should check them out?"

"Depends on what we find in the house," Steinberg said, trying the door. It was locked. He rummaged around in his pocket until he came up with the key the court clerk had sealed in the envelope along with the court order. There was a small round cardboard tag on the key with the house's address scrawled across it.

He slipped the key in the lock, twisted it and turned the knob.

Steinberg caught the full impact of the blow.

A blast of hot air with astonishing force behind it slammed into him. It sent him sprawling backward, tumbling down the short flight of steps. He fell, rolled over in the wet grass and came up on his haunches. There was a small abrasion on the right side of his face and a hole in his pants near his knee.

Carr, who had been standing behind Steinberg when he opened the door, had been propelled to one side and was slumped in the corner between the siding and the porch railing. He was stunned and trying to catch his breath. "What—what the hell was that?"

Steinberg was trying to regain his equalibrium. "Damned if I know. It felt like some kind of explosion."

"Are you okay?" Carr stammered.

Steinberg nodded. "I think so." He stood up, brushed himself off, looked at the door and then at Carr. "I didn't see a damn thing, but I sure as hell felt it."

Carr righted himself and peered through the open door into the murky interior.

Steinberg ascended the steps for a second time. His face was drained of color.

"Are you sure this is necessary?" Carr laughed.

"I can do without another one of those," Steinberg admitted. He worked his way through the door and found himself standing in a hallway adjacent to the kitchen. From there he could see all the way to the front door. Immediately to his left was another door; having studied the layout of the house, he knew it went to the basement. To his right, through an open door, he could see a bathroom; the fixtures were rusty and, for the most part, covered with a dried, thick black coating.

He walked cautiously; the floor could be rotted with debris covering holes. You don't need anymore surprises like that first one, he was telling himself. The sketch of the house's interior was burned into his memory. Up the hall was the living room with a fireplace; next to it was the staircase leading to the upper floor.

Carr was right behind him, eyeing each pile of rubbish and shadow suspiciously. Now he knew why the deputy that had looked into the house the night Bellini was reported missing had conducted such a cursory search. Even in the gray daylight, it was difficult to see. He heard something behind him, wheeled and saw a rat scurry across the hall behind him, disappearing in the gap under the basement door. Carr felt an uncharacteristic prickle in the nape of his neck.

"Damn place smells like a sewer," Steinberg complained.

Carr was trying to imagine what it had been like for the psychic with the infrared cameras that had spent the night in the old house. He had a mental picture of the man and his colleague being completely unnerved by the experience.

Steinberg worked his way through the living room, out onto the enclosed porch, past the bar and circled back. He looked at Carr. "Three floors in all, right?"

"Three plus the basement. There is a sewing room on the second floor. That's the room where they claim all the trouble started."

Steinberg climbed the stairs and methodically worked his way through the rooms on the second floor, noting that the temperature seemed to be dropping as he worked his way from one room to the next. By the time he got to the third floor there was a distinct chill in the air. He saw why. In the room where the two boys, sons of the previous owner, had slept there was an open window. It was raining in, and the damp flooring extended all the way out to the landing at the top of the stairs. Impulsively, he started toward the window to close it. He was halfway across the room when the door slammed shut behind him. Just as quickly, the window fell shut and the room was instantly filled with the stiffling odors of mildew and age.

Steinberg froze. He had the distinct feeling there was someone or something in the room with him. He stood motionless—waiting and listening.

The rotted, decaying curtains moved in an unseen breeze, and he felt a chilling sensation in his legs and back.

The only sound in the room was that of his

own breathing, shallow and accelerated. He backed slowly into a corner, his eyes darting about the room without moving his head.

A picture on the wall next to the window began to rotate slowly, emitting a scraping sound until it hung upside down. It stayed that way for several seconds until it plummeted to the floor, glass shattering, frame splintering.

Steinberg remained motionless. There was a disturbing silence in the room—a void amidst the sound of the rain, the wind and the world. He had no way of knowing that the eerie silence was the prelude to the voice.

He heard it distinctly.

"Leave us alone."

The voice came from within the room, from something that was there in the room with him. The command was little more than a tortured rasp. He would later describe it as agonized and suffering, unlike anything he had ever heard before.

Suddenly he had the feeling that the room was closing in on him. The door opened, slammed shut, opened again and rattled closed. The window began to open and close. A pane of the mullioned glass cracked, shattered and fell to the floor.

Steinberg braced himself, but as suddenly as it began—it stopped.

The door creaked open, and cold air poured into the room. Somehow he knew that whatever force had momentarily held him captive, it was now setting him free.

When he stepped into the hallway, his knees were shaking. He saw Carr standing on the landing halfway between the second and third floors. "What the hell was the commotion?"

Steinberg started down the stairs, brushing past his fellow officer without a response. Carr could see the lack of color in his colleague's face.

"Jesus, Jerry, you look like you've seen a ghost."

Steinberg's reply was terse. "I didn't see it, Stephen, but there's not much doubt in my mind that there's one up there."

At the chancery on Montgomery Street, Alice Chambers sat nervously on the edge of her chair while the two priests conferred in muffled tones. She had already decided that she liked the one called Father Chiraldi better than his counterpart. Father Cannon appeared to be the impatient type; his manner reminded her too much of Monsignor McConnell and made her feel uncomfortable.

After the two men concluded their exchange, Chiraldi looked up and smiled. "The reason for our prolonged discussion, Mrs. Chambers, is that you are the second person to bring this matter to our attention within a matter of days. Is there any chance Lt. Steinberg of the Suffolk County police department asked you to come here?"

Alice shook her head.

"Just yesterday, a Lt. Jerome Steinberg spoke

to us about this very matter. Like you, he was seeking the assistance of the chancery."

"I've—I've met the Lieutenant," the woman admitted, "but he has nothing to do with my being here."

Chiraldi sat down beside her. "The house you speak of," he said softly, "has come to the attention of this office before. Several years ago, the owner of that very same house reported what at the time was thought to be unexplained phenomena. This office advised the gentleman that his needs could best be served by consulting a specialist in the field of parapsychology. Whether the gentleman chose to follow that advice or not is unclear. The matter remained open on our docket for some time, but our records indicate that there were no further inquiries."

"But surely there is something you can do," Alice May insisted.

The older of the two priests leaned back in his chair and tented his fingers. "Just exactly what would you have us do, Mrs. Chambers?" When he leaned forward again, Alice May noticed the document on the desk in front of him.

"I see that you were at one time a member of the Order of the Poor Handmaids, Mrs. Chambers. If that is the case, I feel certain you already understand the procedure for Church intervention in a matter of this nature."

Alice nodded.

Cannon continued. "In addition to being priests, both Father Chiraldi and I are trained papapsychologists. Father Chiraldi is likewise the diocesan-appointed exorcist for this area. However, we are under strict orders not to become envolved in matters of this nature until there is reasonable proof that demonic influences could be at the heart of the matter."

"Demonic influences?" Alice repeated numbly.

"Who would you normally turn to in matters of this nature, Mrs. Chambers," Chiraldi asked.

"Father Bellini," she answered.

Cannon and Chiraldi looked at each other before Cannon continued. "Believe us, Mrs. Chambers, we are sympathetic to your situation. But until someone qualified to do so determines that our involvement is required, I'm afraid that I must deny your request for an investigation by this office."

Chiraldi was still trying. "I see that you are a member of Saint Alomar parrish, Mrs. Chambers. Have you considered discussing this matter with Monsignor McConnell in Father Bellini's absence?"

Alice shook her head. A simple half-truth was better than trying to explain the ongoing friction between the Monsignor and her since she left the order.

"Well then," Cannon grunted, "I believe Father Chiraldi has just pointed out the proper next step."

When Alice got up to leave, Father Chiraldi escorted her to the door and lowered his voice. "If Monsignor McConnell can't help you, give me a call." He pressed a piece of paper into her hand with his telephone number.

Two successive misbehavior reports by Mrs. Camino had plunged Lester into trouble again. As he left the room after his last class of the day and began unwrapping his gum, he was informed that Sister Bertha wanted to see him.

Lester would tell his stepmother that it didn't seem fair that Kooch, who had instigated the latest incident, wasn't there to take his punishment along with him. When Alice Chambers reminded the boy that Donald Webster was home with his grieving mother, Lester felt guilty about his remark. His only consolation was that eventually Kooch would have to face Sister Bertha—dead grandmother or not.

Punishment was decidedly more painful when Sister Bertha metered it out. The heavyset woman had a reputation for being much tougher on the students than the elderly Monsignor. McConnell was content to make wrong-doers say ten rosaries or do five Stations of the Cross. Sister Bertha, on the other hand, delighted in the cruelest punishment of all—calling the student's parents in for a conference.

"So, Lester," the woman hissed, "I see you are on report again."

Lester nodded and shuffled his feet.

"Well, since you seem to be too weak to improve your deportment on the bus, I think we should have your father come in to talk to us."

Lester's heart sank. "Yes, Sister," he said

dutifully. It was the only response Sister Bertha would accept without adding fuel to the fire. "When?"

"Saturday morning at nine."

Minutes later, in the hall outside of Sister Bertha's office, Lester paused just long enough to check his reflection in the mirror. He wondered if the other kids could tell that he had been crying. His father would be furious; another whipping with the belt was a certainty.

Lester need not have worried. The halls were empty. His fellow students had departed, and the school bus was gone. He would have to walk home again. What Lester did notice when he looked in the mirror was the stain; it had started to creep up onto his wrist.

... DAY NINE ...

The doorbell rang in the Chambers household at 8:07. Alice Chambers, still in her housecoat, hurried to the door. She was surprised to see the lieutenant from the Suffolk County police department. His shoulders were hunched against the chilly air, and his collar was buttoned tight against his throat to protect him from the wind. Past him, along the street, she could see wind-blown leaves swirling along the sidewalk.

"Sorry to bother you again, Mrs. Chambers," Steinberg said, "but I was in the neighborhood and had a couple of questions I wanted to ask you."

Alice escorted the officer into the living room, seated him and fixed him a cup of tea. She assumed that Lester had gotten himself into more trouble. She had already received a call from Sister Bertha at Saint Alomar insisting on a Saturday morning conference with her husband. "Is this about Lester?" she asked.

"For the most part," Steinberg said evenly.

"Is he in more trouble?"

Steinberg scowled. "Did your son describe the items he took from the house on Ocean Avenue?"

"He said he took only one thing—a china bowl."

"And that's what he pawned at Silverman's Pawnshop?"

Alice nodded. Now she was wondering if there was something that Lester hadn't told her.

"Does Lester see the Webster boy every day at school?"

"Yes—except of course the last couple of days. Donald has been home with his mother during the bereavement period."

"Did you know Mrs. Cordes?"

"I'd never met her, but I did speak to her on the phone several times."

Steinberg nodded and cleared his throat. "Mrs. Chambers, do you know if your son has been back to the house on Ocean Avenue since last Saturday?"

Alice hesitated. Lester, who had enjoyed a reputation for being honest, had been caught both lying and stealing in the last week; now she couldn't be certain. "I don't believe he has," she said. "His father punished him severely for his last transgression." The moment she said it, she felt as if she had betrayed her husband.

"Under the circumstances, Mrs. Chambers, I think you and your husband should take every precaution to make sure Lester doesn't go back in that house." He did not elaborate nor mention his experience of the previous day.

Alice May's response was an acknowledging nod of the head.

Satisfied that the Chambers family had been duly warned, Steinberg stood up to leave. He offered a smile, "Well, now, that wasn't too painful, was it?"

Steinberg would later describe Alice Chambers' condition as "extremely nervous" in his day log.

The visit with Alice Chambers had taken less time than Steinberg anticipated. He was ahead of schedule. He stopped at the newsstand on Grace, bought a paper and went directly to Field's Bar and Grille on Hawthorne, situating himself, as he usually did, in the last booth. He ordered a cup of coffee and scanned *The Times*; Father Chiraldi wasn't due for another half hour.

While he waited, he slipped his day log out of his pocket and went over his check list, deleting the name of Alice Chambers. When a shadow fell over the table, he looked up. Father Vincent Chiraldi was early.

"Have a seat, Father."

"I'd feel better if you called me Vincent."

Chiraldi smiled, slid into the seat across from him and winked. "Is it too early to have a beer?"

"I've known people to start earlier."

Steinberg had been right. He had reasoned that if he could talk to Chiraldi outside of the chancery and away from his superior, he might make some headway. He waited until the waitress brought the priest his beer before beginning. "Since I talked to you and Father Cannon, I obtained a court order and we've searched the house."

Chiraldi took a couple of hearty swallows and waited.

Steinberg would later admit that he hadn't realized how difficult it would be to talk to another man about a haunted house even though the man was an expert in the field. He allowed that part of his difficulty may have been Chiraldi's demeanor, constantly smiling, charming and attired in a Fordham University sweatshirt. Vincent Chiraldi did not fit Steinberg's concept of a priest.

"So you've been through it, huh?" Chiraldi asked.

"The better part of it."

"Scary?" Chiraldi asked.

Steinberg raised his eyebrows. "How did you know?"

Father Vincent Chiraldi laughed easily. "I'm thirty-eight years old, Lieutenant. I've been in this business almost fifteen years now. At this point, not much surprises me."

"Then you actually believe there could be

something unusual going on in that old house?"
He hesitated to use the word "supernatural."

"Hey, I'm not a skeptic—I'm a believer. Maybe I've never been in that particular house or talked to the former owner, but I've seen others. You won't have a hard time convincing me there's something *extraordinary* going on inside those walls."

"I could hear you stress the word 'extraordinary' when you said it."

Chiraldi leaned back, cradling the bottle between his hands. "That's the rub, Lieutenant. Extraordinary doesn't necessarily mean evil or demonic. Sometimes all we're dealing with is some poor essence that can't find his or her way out of the mess they've gotten themselves into."

"Which means?"

"Meaning your ghost or your essence will probably go away if someone can show them the way."

Steinberg finished his coffee and signaled for a refill. "You're serious about this, aren't you?"

"That's what it's all about. That's what Father Cannon was trying to tell you. The way the Church looks at it, we don't want to get in there and muck up things unless someone can prove that we're dealing with the big bad ass himself."

"How do I take the first step?"

"You bring in some folks who know how to determine what's going on in there. There's a specialist for everything these days. If these folks determine we're dealing with evil forces, that's when Cannon and I get into the act."

"Suppose I needed a name?"

"I can supply names," Chiraldi said. "I just can't go in there until I'm authorized. However, it has to be off the record. Cannon doesn't like it when I bend the rules."

"Off the record," Steinberg assured him. "Where do we start?"

"We start with you telling me what happened yesterday. Tell me everything. Don't leave anything out, no matter how insignificant you may think it is."

Steinberg leaned forward to begin, but as he did, Chiraldi held up his hand.

"Wait—I'll get more out of this if I have another beer before you start."

Alice Chambers had a busy day. Steinberg's unexpected visit caused her to be late picking up Lester for the 10:30 appointment with Dr. Lawrence Spielmann. She had to drive the boy to a medical complex on Euclid in Farmingdale.

Spielmann examined Lester's hand and wrist and checked his general physical condition, then he left the room. A nurse came in a few minutes later, asked Alice a number of questions about her stepson's physical and emotional condition, and then took tissue samples with a small instrument that reminded her of a hypodermic needle. Then they were instructed to wait in Spielmann's office.

When Spielmann came back into the room there was a perplexed look on his face. "When Dr. Crispman called me, he indicated that he had made a preliminary diagnosis of lentigo maligna melanoma. After seeing Lester, I don't believe that's what we're dealing with."

Alice did not know whether to be encouraged or discouraged by what the man said. To her way of thinking, there were afflictions worse than skin cancer; after all, there were effective treatments that could rid the boy of it. Now, not knowing what they were dealing with was every bit as unsettling as Crispman's original diagnosis.

"I'll know a lot more after we've had the opportunity to work up the tissue samples, Mrs. Chambers. In the meantime, we'll just have to keep our fingers crossed."

What Alice said then surprised her as much as it did the doctor. "I have something better than crossed fingers, Dr. Spielmann. I have prayer."

At the Rockmeyer Funeral Home on Coalsprings Road, Alice Chambers met Charla Webster for the first time. The viewing room was small. In all, there were eight people present. Lester talked briefly to Kooch, and Charla thanked Alice May for the flowers from the Chambers family. It was Thursday, October 21st, and services for Jacalyn Cordes were to be held at 9:00 A.M. on Saturday morning.

At 1:15, Alice Chambers dropped Lester off at Saint Alomar with a note for Sister Bertha confirming their 9:00 A.M. appointment on Saturday morning. She then drove around the corner to see if Monsignor McConnell could spend a few minutes with her. Later that day she would make the following entry in her journal: *"I wanted to talk to him about the images. They have become more and more distressing."*

At the rectory, Mrs. Heart informed her that Monsignor McConnell was continuing his fast and was unavailable. She also informed Alice that there had been no further word regarding Father Bellini.

At the Suffolk County police department, Jerome Steinberg sat across from Sara Wine, listening to the truant officer's assessment of Donald Webster and Lester Chambers. She had just completed a two day review of the records of the two boys at Steinberg's request.

"The Webster boy's records are messy, but they're pretty straightforward. What you see is what you get. Parents divorced, the boy has been overindulged and undersupervised for years. We call it the old climbing parent's syndrome. He was in trouble constantly when he was at Precious Blood. The truth of the matter is, I don't see much difference in his behavior pattern between then and now. He was a problem back at Precious Blood in Brooklyn as well. Which brings me to my question—why are you so interested in these two?"

"Remember those books your deputy found at the old house on Ocean Avenue? The ones you gave me that morning?"

Sara nodded.

"Well, these same two kids keep turning up—in the Silverman case, the Bellini matter. Every time I turn around, I find another thread that leads me directly to these two boys."

"Are you telling me you think they actually had something to do with the murder of Leon Silverman?"

"Sounds farfetched, doesn't it?" Steinberg admitted.

"Well, nothing surprises me these days. But from what I've read, whoever killed Silverman had to be awfully strong to pin him to the wall and then drive that thing through his chest."

Steinberg got up, walked around his desk and stared out at the gray October day.

"Look, Jerry, you don't pull someone's records without digging up a little dirt along the way. I did hear some gossip about the Chambers family that I'd want to check into further before I started spreading it around as gospel."

Steinberg turned and stared at the woman. "Let's hear it."

"It sounds as though Roy Chambers and his first wife had more than their share of ups and downs. Enough so on one occasion he considered filing for divorce."

"On what grounds?"

"Infidelity."

"But he didn't go through with it?"

Sara shook her head. "Apparently someone talked him out of it."

"Go on."

"It seems Roy Chambers was in a terrible accident shortly after his daughter was born."

"And?"

"He was busted up pretty good. Certain delicate operations were performed." Sara appeared to be blushing. "Do I have to draw you pictures?"

"Apparently—what are you getting at?"

"Bottom line, no more children since some of the critical plumbing was disconnected. The way the story was told to me—the doctors told Chambers, but Chambers never told his wife. So, two years later when the lady turns up pregnant, Roy Chambers' suspicions about his wife's infidelity are confirmed."

"Now comes the divorce, right?"

"Wrong. A little over a year later, after the baby arrived, the first Mrs. Chambers committed suicide. It doesn't go anywhere from there except that I've been told by a couple of the nuns over at Saint Alomar that Lester Chambers frequently shows up at school with a pretty good assortment of cuts and bruises."

"Do you read it that the old man is taking it out on the boy?" Steinberg asked.

Sara nodded. "It's right out of the textbooks," she confirmed.

"Then this Mrs. Chambers is the second wife, correct?"

"Correct. And Lester Chambers is a confused little boy living in a house with a man who didn't father him, doesn't love him, and a stepmother who probably doesn't know anything about all of this. Even if she does, it's my guess she doesn't know what to do about it."

That afternoon, in the quiet of the empty house, Alice May retired to her button room to make the following entry in her journal:

"The dream is a recurring one, but each time it seems to be more intense and more terrifying. I do not recognize the house or the individual in the dream, but I know that the tortured soul comes to me seeking my intervention.

"The woman's face is fair, but she looks exhausted. Her skin and her hair are lifeless. She carries the child in her arms with the same tender care that I see new mothers exhibit at Mass. When I approach, she holds the child out for me to see. She peels the coverlet back from the infant's face, and I recoil.

"It is a vision more hideous than words can describe. It is red and swollen, and the eyes are those of something sinister. It smiles, exhibiting its mouth full of sharp, jagged teeth. It hisses like a serpent, and I realize that it is the most evil countenance I have ever looked upon.

"'My sin,' the woman says. 'This is my sin. Until it is destroyed I cannot know peace.'

"I try to console her, but I avoid looking at the child/thing. It is fiendish, an instrument

of unspeakable evil. I know that I can help so I reach for her burden, but she pulls away.

"The stench of that vile thing is overwhelming. I am powerless. My eyes bore into the creature's eyes, and we are locked in mortal combat—a combat I know I cannot win.

"In that tiny yet intractable face, I see unspeakable evil, and my soul screams out in anguish and terror.

"I crumple to the floor, knowing that I have been face to face with the Prince of Darkness."

That Thursday evening, Roy Chambers came home from work to find his wife crouched in the corner of her button room. In her hands she held what was left of one of Ellen's dolls. Alice's hands were bleeding. She had clawed the face off of the tiny marionette and disgorged it's eyes.

He assisted his wife into the bedroom and gave her a sleeping pill. As she slipped into her world of troubled sleep, he heard her say, "I will destroy it."

... DAY TEN ...

Jerome Steinberg was awakened by the incessant ringing of the telephone. He groped about in the clutter on his nightstand until he located the receiver and picked it up. "Steinberg here."

"Jerry, it's me, Vincent."

Steinberg threw back the covers and sat up. He grunted into the mouthpiece to let Chiraldi know he was listening while he put on his glasses and checked the clock. He had overslept. It was 7:10, Friday, October 22nd.

"Have you ever heard of the Messatos?" Chiraldi asked.

"Messato?" Steinberg repeated. "The name doesn't ring a bell."

"Actually, there's two of them. Vito is an old fraternity brother of mine; his wife's name is

135

Carolyn. I was talking to them last night and told them about your investigation. Vito seemed to be pretty interested. Bottom line, he offered their assistance."

Steinberg was still half-asleep. "What kind of assistance?"

"Vito is a parapsychologist and does some investigative work for the police in Queens. Not only that, his wife is a psychic. They've heard about the house in Amityville."

Steinberg had mixed emotions. He wanted help, but he was reluctant to get outsiders involved. He did not want to be accused of turning the Bellini investigation into another three-ring circus similar to the one a decade earlier. Still, he had ask Chiraldi for help, and now the priest was offering it.

"It's all set up, Jerry. All you have to do is call Vito and tell him when and where you want to meet him."

"How about dragging you along?"

"I was afraid you weren't going to ask. Call Vito, then call me back; just tell me where and when."

Steinberg wrote down the Messato phone number, thanked Chiraldi and promised to call him back within the hour. Then he headed for the shower.

In the Chambers household, Roy Chambers was preparing to leave for work. The lines in his wife's face showed the effects of her troubled night. Over her husband's admonitions to rest, she prepared Ellen and Lester's breakfast and helped them off to school.

Fifteen minutes before Roy was scheduled to leave for his train, he sat down with his wife. "About last night . . ." He hesitated.

Alice May took a sip of coffee and tried to dismiss the incident with a nonchalant wave of her hand. "I don't know what got into me. When I came home from the funeral home, I felt very depressed."

Reluctant to bring up the subject of the mutilated doll, Roy approached the matter from a different perspective. "Is there something going on with Lester that I don't know about?"

The question caught Alice by surprise. When she hesitated, her husband assumed the worst.

"Is it Lester?" he repeated. "Is Lester behind all of this?"

Alice shook her head. She had not told anyone about the dream that had been recurring for the past eight days. She had intended to tell Father Bellini, but Bellini never showed up at the Chambers house that day. She had made two attempts to talk to Monsignor McConnell about the vision, but McConnell continued his fast and was still unavailable. "No, it's not Lester," she said.

"Well, if it is Lester, I don't want you protecting him. I know how to put that young man in his place. A good thrashing seems to be about the only thing that gets that boy's attention."

Roy did not hear his wife's response. His quick temper had already taken over. His face was red, and Alice May knew it was pointless to try to reason with the man until the anger had passed. She decided there was no way to clear up the matter until he returned home that evening after his usual Friday night bowling league.

"Now I hear we've got a conference with Sister Bertha tomorrow morning," he fumed. "If it isn't one thing with that kid, it's another."

Alice May was relieved when her husband hurriedly glanced at his watch and realized it was time to leave. He was still pulling out of the driveway when she picked up the telephone to call the Saint Alomar rectory. She was desperate to talk to someone about the vision in her dreams, and the only person left to her, with Father Bellini gone, was the Monsignor.

At the parish house, Mrs. Heart answered the phone.

"This is Alice Chambers. I must speak to the Monsignor." Alice May would question in her journal if the housekeeper could hear the desperation in her voice.

Virginia Heart was a robust woman in her late fifties. She had been the housekeeper at the Saint Alomar rectory since her husband passed away some 18 years earlier. It was said that no one was more critical of the aging priest than Mrs. Heart. It was also said that the woman firmly believed she was the only one that was entitled to criticize McConnell. She staunchly defended him when anyone else tried to do so.

To the outsider, Virginia Heart spoke of David McConnell in only the most glowing of terms.

Alice received the same message she had for the past several days. Monsignor McConnell was continuing his fast, and the best the housekeeper could do was relay her message—if and when the opportunity presented itself.

"I was also wondering if there has been any word on Father Bellini?"

"We've heard nothing," Mrs. Heart informed her.

When Alice hung up, she was more disturbed than ever. She still had no one with whom she could discuss her distressing dream.

At the Rockmeyer Funeral Home on Coalsprings Road, Gerald Harrison, the manager of the facility, was preparing for another busy day. When he unlocked the door to the parlor's entrance, he was confronted by Charla Webster, her son, Donald, and Mrs. Webster's aunt, a woman by the name of Clara Morrison. He suggested that if they would wait until he turned on the lights in the foyer, he would escort them to the West Room where the body of Jacalyn Cordes was to be viewed.

As the small entourage entered the west wing, the phone rang and Gerald Harrison went to answer it, uncharacteristically sending Charla Webster and her family on ahead. A few minutes later, he stated that he found the two women standing in the middle of the Cordes viewing room. Both women were hysterical. The 11-year-old boy was standing beside his mother, looking frightened and confused. All of the flower arrangements had withered and turned black, as though they had been frozen.

At the Suffolk County police department, Stephen Carr was reviewing the Silverman file. The assisting officer, Sgt. Alfred Hammond, was sitting across the desk from him. Hammond, like Carr, was a long time veteran of the department.

Carr looked up from the file and took off his half glasses. "Okay, I've read it. It's all nice and official. But I know you well enough, Al, to ask what you didn't put in the report—your hunches."

Hammond was a taciturn man who gave nonverbal responses to most questions. Carr was one of the few people who could dig this sort of information out of him. "I haven't had a chance to get with Jerry Steinberg yet."

"I'm not asking you what Steinberg thinks; I want to know what you think."

Hammond began in his usual manner, slowly, with long ungainly pauses between words. "It's —hard to figure. When Gloria Peranson came into the station, it was damn near two o'clock in the morning. She had already been out to her father's place and couldn't rouse him. She and her husband drove back in and insisted we send someone out with them to break into the house."

"Doesn't it seem curious to you that she would come here instead of calling for help?"

"Hey, what can I say? She was rattled."

"And Fredricks went out to the old man's house with her?"

"He was the one on duty. It's all in his log. He arrived at the Silverman residence at half past two. The Peranson woman told him she had received a call from her father about ten o'clock the previous evening. She said he was upset, and then she heard him scream. Well, the first thing they did was try to call some of his cronies to have them go over and check on him, but they couldn't reach anyone. So they jumped in their car and drove down to Amityville to check it out."

"All the way from Westover?"

"That's what she said."

"Why didn't they call the police from Westover to have us check it out?"

"Hell, Stephen, I don't know. Like I said, she was rattled."

"According to Fredricks' report all the doors were locked."

"Not only locked, dead-bolted. Fredricks made sure I understood that when I got there. By the time you and Jerry got there I had checked it all out; all the windows were locked and there were no signs of forced entry."

"According to your report we didn't find any fingerprints."

"None. Zippo. Nothing in the bedroom and nothing on the murder weapon either."

141

"Motive?"

"Who knows with a pawnbroker? One thing we do know, it wasn't theft. There was four thousand dollars and change in the drawer in the nightstand beside the bed. The killer didn't touch it. In fact, there's nothing to indicate the killer even looked for anything."

Carr grunted and began rifling through a stack of 8 by 10's from the police lab. He paused when he came to the picture of Silverman's dead cat. "Why this?"

"I thought it was curious, that's all. You know, we find a guy murdered, and his cat's dead, too. I had Griminski take a picture of it."

"How did the newspapers get it?"

"Beats me. Ask Griminski."

"Okay, one more time. What aren't you telling me?"

Hammond hesitated. "Well—like I said, I ain't had a chance to get with Steinberg yet, but—"

"But what?"

"I had an autopsy run on the cat. Call it a long shot. I had a gut feeling. There was this dead cat laying next to a funny-looking bowl. I wondered if it had been poisoned."

"Was it?"

"Are you ready for this? The cat died of a heart attack."

Carr sagged back in his chair. He studied Hammond for a moment then reached in his desk drawer and produced a large manila envelope. "Here, read this."

Hammond reached across the desk and picked up the envelope.

"It's the autopsy report on Leon Silverman. I'll save you the trouble of reading it. It says that the official cause of death of Leon Silverman is a heart attack. That wood auger would have killed him, but the coroner thinks Silverman died moments before his assailant screwed that thing through his chest."

After Hammond left his office, Carr pulled the Bellini file out of the cabinet and placed it next to the Silverman folder.

He drew columns and began to make notes. First there was Bellini. McConnell's assistant had been at Saint Alomar for five years. For all practical purposes, he was a local boy. His mother still lived in Massapequa, and Bellini had grown up in the area. His whereabouts up until the time of his disappearance was a matter of record, and the record was well-documented. The fact that he left the church's black Ford Fairmont where he did was the only surprise. Steinberg had traced Bellini from the CYO field to his mother's house and twice verified Bellini's intention to show up at the Chambers house that afternoon.

There were two aspects of the Bellini disappearance that bothered Carr. Steinberg was reasonably certain that Joseph Bellini had been seeing a woman by the name of Judith Brewer— and Judith Brewer had last been seen two months prior to Bellini's disappearance. Judith

Brewer left no forwarding address, and Steinberg had been unable to locate anyone who had talked to her since she walked out of the insurance office where she was employed on a Friday afternoon in August.

The lab report on Father Bellini's car however seemed to counter the willful disappearance theory. The interior of Bellini's car was splattered with blood—O positive. Records showed that Bellini had O positive blood.

Carr lay the Bellini file aside and turned back to the Silverman case. So far, his investigation had raised as many questions as it had answered. He leafed through the voluminous report for the third time that day and noted the yellow highlighting over key phrases—"no fingerprints," "no evidence of forced entry," "no apparent motive."

Lastly, there was the Jacalyn Cordes accident. He glanced at the Xerox copy of the summary report. Jerome Steinberg, a cop he respected, insisted on weaving the death of the Cordes woman into the fabric of the bizarre puzzle. Carr wasn't so sure.

By his own definition, Carr was not a superstitious man. He did not believe in ghosts, nor did he have much faith in long odds. For the moment, he viewed the Cordes accident as nothing more than an intriguing coincidence. He was, however, a cautious and prudent man who tried to keep an open mind. Facts were facts. Leon Silverman had been found with a wood auger driven through his chest. That wood auger was stolen from the house on Ocean Avenue. The missing priest's car was found in the driveway of the same house. And Jacalyn Cordes was the grandmother of one of the boys who had been stealing from that same house.

Chance?

Coincidence?

Or was something else involved?

It occurred to Carr that he would not even be considering the involvement of "something else" if the whole scenario did not revolve around a house where bizarre happenings had been reported in the past.

He put the files back in his desk and went looking for Steinberg. Then he remembered that Steinberg had told him he was headed for Queens to meet the Messatos.

Father Vincent Chiraldi introduced Jerome Steinberg to Vito and Carolyn Messato in a small second floor apartment late that afternoon. Chiraldi and his former fraternity brother exchanged small talk, Vito showing the priest snapshots of his two-year-old son, Anthony. Eventually the conversation turned to the reason for their meeting.

Several times during his subsequent taping sessions with John Kelly, Steinberg alluded to the difficulty in describing what he and Carr encountered during their first investigation into the house on Ocean Avenue. But, as in his earlier conversation with Chiraldi, when that barrier was overcome, the details came spilling out.

Carolyn Messato, a short, heavyset woman in her late thirties, possessed probing eyes and a gentle smile. She proved to be a careful listener, picking up on even on the slightest change in speech patterns. Steinberg was later to learn that she was the one who would establish the contact. Carolyn Messato was a medium.

"Do I sense that you do not believe in the existence of another realm?" Carolyn asked.

Steinberg admitted that he didn't, but added that he was less confident of his answer now than he had been a few days earlier. The admission brought smiles from both Vito Messato and Father Chiraldi.

"You realize, of course, what my position is in this matter, Vito. Officially I'm not even here. I can't do anything for the Lieutenant here until someone with the right credentials makes an assessment of the place. Once that's accomplished—and if there is reason to believe we actually have some sort of demonic involvement—I'll get Father Cannon involved, too."

"Do you believe there is such a thing as demonic involvement, Lieutenant?" Carolyn asked.

Steinberg refused to answer.

"Don't be embarrassed, Lieutenant," Vito said. "Some of the terminology takes a little getting used to. What Carolyn is really asking is, based on what you believe you saw and heard the other day, did you have the feeling that the influence in that room with you was evil in nature?"

"Or," Carolyn interjected, "did you get the feeling that you were simply unwelcome?"

"I had the feeling that whoever or whatever was there in the room with me wanted me out of there."

Carolyn smiled. "Very good. Now we're getting somewhere. In other words, Lieutenant, you sensed hostility?"

Steinberg nodded. "What if I told you it was more like some kid having a temper tantrum—windows going up and down, doors slamming and opening—"

"Perhaps it was a child. We all know that children can be very rude, and the essence of a rude child will be every bit as rude or spoiled as its real world counterpart."

"You must understand, Lieutenant," Vito clarified, "essence, spirit, ghost are all, for the most part, interchangeable terms in our profession. We seldom use the term 'ghost' because it has come to have a somewhat childish connotation. Nevertheless, a ghost is a ghost is a ghost."

"Let me explain something, Jerry," Chiraldi said. "It's entirely possible that all four of us could drive out to that house tonight and there would be no manifestation of the phenomena you encountered earlier. Or it might appear to only one of us and not the rest of us. It all depends."

"That's part of the problem. I experienced it; Carr didn't. He didn't see what I saw or feel the fluctuations in temperature—none of that. Outside of feeling the hot air blast at the back door, he saw and felt none of it—although he did hear the noise when I was on the third floor."

"Let me ask you, Lieutenant, do you think your associate believed you when you told him what happened?" Carolyn asked.

Steinberg hesitated.

"Let me put it another way," she pressed. "If your colleague had told you what you told him, would you have believed him?"

Steinberg looked at the woman. "No," he said flatly.

"We're making progress," she said. "You see, Lieutenant, that's the difference between us and your fellow officer; we believe you. Vito and I both know that it is entirely possible that you have had an encounter with someone or something from the other realm."

"What do you think that someone or something is?"

"We have no way of knowing, Lieutenant, until we look into it. And even then it's possible we won't come up with any answers. Should I assume you want us to begin as soon as possible?"

"The sooner the better."

"What's wrong with this weekend?" Vito asked.

* * *

THE NIGHTMARE CONTINUES

Alice Chambers made her confession, completed her penance and left the sanctuary. Despite the confessional's traditional cloak of secrecy, she was certain she recognized the priest as the same one brought in by Saint Alomar to substitute for the then-ailing Father Bellini a year earlier.

From the sanctuary, she walked across the courtyard to the academy and stood in the hallway waiting for the last bell that dismissed classes for the day. When she spotted Lester racing for the bus and stuffing his mouth full of gum, she intercepted the boy and offered him a ride home.

Lester was more animated than usual and decidedly more verbal. Sister Bertha had spent a great deal of time that day in catechism class dealing with the subject of death and the afterlife. Alice assumed it was the school's way of helping the youngsters understand what Donald Webster was experiencing with the death of his grandmother. Alice did not know that it was because Lester had insisted on talking about the existence of ghosts.

Leaving Glencoe, she turned off of Meyer Road onto Ocean Avenue. As they neared the old house, Lester pressed her to drive slowly and roll her window down. When she asked him why, Lester told her that he wanted her to see that he and Kooch had not done anything really bad to the old house.

* * *

149

Later that evening, after Roy Chambers had arrived home and retired for the evening, Alice Chambers closed the door to her button room and made a troubled entry in her journal:

"I know now where the vision comes from. I could feel its presence when we drove past the house.

"There are evil forces with unfathomable powers at work within that house.

"Oh, most merciful Savior, pray for the salvation of my soul and assist me in my struggle to turn back these forces of darkness."

... DAY ELEVEN ...

Gerald Harrison was ready. In an interview with John Kelly, he would state that he had been anxious to wrap up the Cordes service because of the series of strange events that occurred in the Rockmeyer Funeral Home during that period. First there had been the incident with the black flowers, explained, Harrison believed, by a malfunctioning air conditioner. The second night of the Cordes viewing, Harrison found it necessary to curtail viewing and closed early because of unpleasant odors throughout the facility. A plumber worked throughout the night to find the cause of the odor but could find none. The next morning the smell was inexplicably gone. Harrison, likewise, did not have an explanation for the organ music reported by the night janitor. The man insisted that someone was in the chapel playing the organ in the middle of the night. Harrison was carrying the only key to the locked chapel, and the janitor was unable to verify the source of the music.

Now the organ was playing again. This time, however, there was an organist at the keyboard, and the services for Jacalyn Cordes were about to begin.

The nondenominational minister walked to the lectern and looked over the small assemblage of mourners.

The guest register for the Rockmeyer Funeral Home included the names of Charla Webster, her son, Donald, and two of Mrs. Webster's aunts, Clara Morrison and Marlene Tillson. There were also four representatives of the First Church of Christ in Bay Shore where Mrs. Cordes had been a lifelong member. The organist was Mrs. Dorothy Comer who regularly served as organist for the Rockmeyer Funeral Home.

About this service, Charla Webster would state that she felt the Church had deserted both her and her mother. No one from the Saint Alomar community attended the service. Charla had embraced the Roman Catholic faith when she had married Donald's father. Her conversion to a faith her mother did not approve of was still a matter of contention between the two women at the time of Mrs. Cordes' death.

THE NIGHTMARE CONTINUES

The minister, Reverend Paul Anglin, began reading from the Twenty-Third Psalm and was just starting to gesture to the open casket when the lights went out. The heavily draped room was plunged into total darkness.

Gerald Harrison, who had been standing in the rear of the West Room when Reverend Anglin began, recalled that the lights had failed on two previous occasions, both times during violent thunderstorms. On the Saturday morning of the Cordes funeral, the sky was overcast and the weather was cold, but there were no reports of thunderstorms.

The moment Harrison was able to determine that it was not a fuse and that the power was out throughout the building, he returned to the chapel with a box of candles. He lit them and placed them around the room, then he apologized to the mourners and appealed to the minister to continue.

Only then did the people in the room realize that the casket, in that brief period of darkness, had somehow been closed.

Harrison summoned an assistant, and for the next several minutes the two men struggled to reopen the casket. The lock was finally broken, and the lid, constructed of heavy textured metal, was repositioned. Harrison glanced down, anticipating that he might have to rearrange the Cordes woman's clothing prior to the viewing following the service. His startled reflex was obvious to everyone in the room.

Jacalyn Cordes' body had turned over inside the casket. The woman was laying face down, her hands entangled in her hair, much of which had been torn out by the roots.

Lester would recall that Kooch told him, "I'll bet she woke up inside the coffin, saw she was trapped and tried to get out."

Several weeks later, the bookkeeper for the Rockmeyer Funeral Home would point out to Gerald Harrison that the power company had rectified a billing error, acknowledging the power failure that had interrupted the service.

At Saint Alomar Academy, at the same time that the Cordes services were being conducted, Roy and Alice Chambers listened to an irate Sister Bertha describe a litany of Lester's behavior and academic problems. In addition to being reported for consistent misbehavior on the school bus, Lester was also portrayed as a student performing below the satisfactory level in three of his six subjects. Sister Bertha complained that Lester had repeatedly been absent when student roll call was taken following morning Mass at the start of the school day.

"If this pattern continues," Sister Bertha announced, "I will have no choice but to put Lester on three day suspension from the Academy. And until I see evidence of Lester trying to improve his deportment, he will not be permitted to ride the school bus."

Alice stared past the portly nun, avoiding her eyes. Nor was it necessary for her to look at her husband since she knew he was outraged at what the woman was telling him.

Sister Bertha closed the file. "I'm sorry," she said, "but we cannot continue to ignore Lester's poor performance any longer. I am just as disappointed in Lester as you are."

Roy Chamber's voice was hard and uncompromising. "I can assure you, Sister Bertha, you will see a decided improvement in Lester's behavior come Monday morning."

The Mother Superior stood up and escorted the couple to the door where another couple was waiting for their 9:30 appointment.

"These sessions are most unfortunate, Mr. Chambers." All of Sister Bertha's remarks were directed at him, ignoring the presence of Alice May. "I would be remiss in my duties if I did not bring these matters to your attention." She shook hands with them, managed an empty smile, ushered the waiting couple into her office and closed the door.

Roy Chambers walked in angry silence. Alice May followed. She knew that it was only a matter of time until the rage manifested itself, and she was helpless to defuse it.

In the rectory, Mrs. Heart fretted with the small tray she was about to carry into the Monsignor's study. The man had lost weight, was suffering from severe headaches and was experiencing difficulty with his breathing. He complained of swollen joints and severe cramps. Still, he persisted in his fast. He would, he informed his housekeeper, reject this tray as he had all the others; he would take nothing to alleviate his discomfort.

Mrs. Heart was grateful to hear however that he intended to terminate his fast at sunset on Sunday. That, she calculated, was less than 32 hours away.

In the Chambers residence at 3257 Oak Street, Roy Chambers brooded about his son's behavior until he decided on the appropriate punishment. He went to the second floor bedroom with the belt that Lester had stolen. Lester was instructed to disrobe and grab hold of the bed railing. Consistent with past practice, Roy administered a beating, the severity of which far exceeded the bounds of prudent parental correction. The whipping lasted a full five minutes. The belt buckle cut deep gashes in the 11-year-old's buttocks and thighs. Lester responded to the barbaric treatment as he knew his father would want him to respond—in stoic silence.

Alice recorded in her journal that her husband did not assuage his anger, but that the punishment was terminated only because the man was too exhausted to continue. Wet with sweat, Roy placed the belt back on the shelf in his closet and instructed Lester to kneel down beside his bed and pray to learn to behave better. From there Roy went to his reading room and did not emerge until late in the day.

Alice bathed and dressed her stepson's wounds, gave him a pillow to kneel on and checked on him at frequent intervals throughout the afternoon.

At 6:00 P.M., Roy, fresh from a shower, went downstairs and inquired what his wife was planning for dinner. When she told him, he advised her to set the table for three. "Lester," he announced, "will not be allowed to dine with the family until Sister Bertha informs us that there has been a decided improvement in his grades and deportment."

Several blocks away, in the Webster household, Charla Webster and her two aunts conducted a wake for Jacalyn Cordes. The funeral was over. The period of mourning had begun. Donald Webster was not with them. He had asked to be excused, telling his mother that he wanted to go for a walk to be alone.

He would later tell Lester that he went to the kennel behind the house at 112 Ocean Avenue and brought home several of the items he had removed from the old house before his grandmother died.

. . . DAY TWELVE . . .

Sunday, October 24th, was a raw, wintery day when Jerome Steinberg stepped from his apartment complex and got into his car. He was headed for a meeting with Vito and Carolyn Messato at 112 Ocean Avenue. During his journey, he recorded his thoughts on a small tape recorder, an instrument he intended to conceal in his pocket so that he could record Carolyn Messato's comments while she made her assessment of the house. If Chiraldi was correct about the woman's abilities, Steinberg believed that Carolyn Messato was likely to come up with information he needed—and he wanted it on tape.

When he pulled into the Ocean Avenue driveway, Vito Messato was just getting out of his blue and gray Ford van. Carolyn Messato was already standing on the front porch of the house, peering through the grimy windows.

Chiraldi was not with them.

Seeing Steinberg, Carolyn came down off the porch and suggested that they get started. Vito unloaded several small boxes of gear from his van. He was carrying two cameras, both loaded with infrared film.

Steinberg led them to the rear of the house and paused long enough to allow the couple to inspect the kennel and boathouse. Carolyn was particularly intrigued by the boathouse and inquired if she could inspect the interior.

She examined the padlock and turned to Steinberg. "With all of the court-ordered 'no trespassing' signs, Lieutenant, I'm surprised these buildings aren't locked."

Steinberg examined it. She was right. On his previous visit, the kennel had been open and the boathouse locked. Now the situation was reversed. He made a note in his day log.

While Carolyn inspected the boathouse, Steinberg studied the footprints in the soft earth around the kennel. They were small, obviously those of a child, and led in and out of the kennel. He suspected that one or both of the boys had disregarded their parents' warning and returned to the house.

When he looked up, he realized that Vito was watching him. "Intruders, Lieutenant?"

Steinberg briefly explained the situation involving the recent thefts.

"Well, Lieutenant," Vito said, "I can assure you, those particular tracks weren't made by a ghost—if you were wondering."

Steinberg was convinced he knew exactly what the tracks were and who made them. He went into the kennel and made an inventory of the items stored along the wall—a carved, silver candelabra, a set of cast, probably bronze bookends, a toolbox and a hand-painted porcelain tea service. From there, he went back to the boathouse and found Carolyn with her eyes closed, standing at the door with her hand on the knob. Vito cautioned him not to speak.

When the woman opened her eyes, she smiled. "Well, Lieutenant, you were right about one thing—we are not welcome."

Steinberg and Messato followed the woman out of the boathouse, across the yard and up to the rear door. She opened it and entered, the two men following. By the time both men had worked their way to the middle of the house, Carolyn had wandered off by herself.

"What's going on?" Steinberg whispered.

"Let her go," Vito said. "She's getting herself oriented. She calls it 'dialing in.'"

On the enclosed porch, Steinberg watched the woman assume a rigid stance with her hands clenched tightly at her side. Her eyes were closed, and her lips moved silently as though she was talking to herself.

Vito quietly explained what was happening. "First thing we intend to determine is whether or not you and your friend were the victims of some kind of fraud or hoax. Secondly, we have to be sure you didn't unconsciously will some of the things that happened."

"How the hell could I will doors slamming and windows going up and down?" Steinberg said.

"Relax, Lieutenant, I said 'unconsciously.' You wouldn't be the first person who walked into a house like this expecting something to happen and had your subconscious take over."

Steinberg revealed in one of his taping sessions that he came close to telling Vito Messato he had never heard of anything so preposterous. Instead, he used the word "impossible."

"I'm afraid it's altogether possible, Lieutenant; you wouldn't be the first, and you won't be the last. The mind can be a powerful instrument in situations like this. As soon as Carolyn is convinced there is evidence of other-realm activity, we can get on with our investigation."

Steinberg remembers that at that point he was both upset and angry. He was a rational man; he knew what he saw, and he knew what he heard. Why did the Messatos insist on being so skeptical. "Damn it, Vito, I didn't imagine it—and I sure as hell didn't will it. Let's get on with it."

Messato smiled. "Remember, Lieutenant, you came to us. We didn't come to you. Trust us; we've been through this before. Now, why don't you let us do it our way."

Steinberg had just taken out his cigarettes when Carolyn walked back into the room. She was shaking her head as her husband unpacked a small, gray valise. "Tape recorder," he said, holding it up for Steinberg's inspection. "Actually, it's a great deal more sensitive than the one you have in your pocket."

Steinberg recalls that he made the mistake of feigning innocence, and Messato informed him that his wife had picked up on the fact that he was carrying a voice-activated tape recorder the moment he got out of his car.

"I know what you're thinking, Lieutenant. Actually, your reactions are pretty much par for the course for someone watching us work for the first time. But you'll have to turn your recorder off. It could distract Carolyn. I'll have one going. Believe me, we won't miss anything."

Steinberg apologized.

"Well?" Vito asked, looking at his wife.

"The Lieutenant was right. There is clearly a presence."

A tour of the rooms on the second and third floors yielded nothing. Vito instructed Steinberg to show the woman where and how he was standing when the occurrence took place. Then he was asked to point out where Stephen Carr was at the same time.

Each time, the woman went to the precise spot, closed her eyes and appeared to lapse into a trance.

At that point, Carolyn descended the stairs, walked past the two men and went to the door leading to the basement. In a voice barely audible, Steinberg heard Carolyn tell her husband that she had established contact.

When Vito opened the basement door, they were assailed by a choking stench. Vito switched on his recorder, reached in his pocket and handed Steinberg a small Minnox camera. "You keep this camera trained on Carolyn, and I'll do the rest."

At the bottom of the steps the odor was so strong that Steinberg's eyes teared. He held one hand over his mouth and kept the camera poised with the other. In the darkness there was nothing but confusion; the floor was littered with debris, and he tripped repeatedly. Vito played the strong beam of the flashlight back and forth across the room, stopping from time to time to check on his wife.

Carolyn was standing in the middle of the room with her arms at her sides and her eyes closed. "Under the stairwell, to the back, you will find a small door," she informed Vito. "Open it."

Steinberg thought that the woman's voice sounded somewhat detached, as though she wasn't the one that had actually spoken the words.

Vito crouched down and inched his way into the tiny room. He groped along the barrier until he found a way to work his fingers behind the panel. He tugged at the barrier with his free hand until the panel peeled away to reveal a bright orange-red glow. Steinberg caught only a brief glimpse of something crouched at the back of the tiny enclosure before Carolyn screamed.

"Shut it, Vito, hurry!"

The crouched Vito released his hold on the panel and leaped. Steinberg caught the full force of Messato's stocky body as the man crashed into him and propelled him backward. Simultaneously, the room was rocked by an explosion. Steinberg hit the floor, rolled over and ended up on his hands and knees. The room was instantly engulfed in flames with Carolyn standing stoically in the middle of the inferno.

"Get the policeman out of here," she ordered.

Vito jerked Steinberg to his feet and shoved him toward the stairs. "You heard her. Get out of here!"

The basement was filled with acrid, choking smoke. Out of the corner of his eye, Steinberg saw flames leaping up all around him. He bolted through the door at the top of the steps, ricocheted off the wall in the hallway and raced for the back door. He could feel Vito right behind him. He leaped from the porch and sprawled face first in the wet grass. He heard Vito hit the ground and then the sound of the man's heavy breathing beside him. He rolled over and started to get up but Vito caught him by the arm. "For God's sake, don't go back in there."

"But your wife is still in there," Steinberg protested.

Still struggling, he saw Carolyn emerge through the rear door. Her face was an ashen gray, and her eyes were glazed.

"Don't touch her," Vito yelled. "Leave her alone."

The woman's face slowly contorted into a grotesque mask, and she hissed at Steinberg like a snake. A forked tongue began darting in and out of her twisted mouth. The hideous action was repeated over and over.

Steinberg recoiled. The hissing sound was followed by a screeching catlike cry and a guttural moan. The light fixture on the porch over the woman's head exploded, and the porch flooring began to buckle and undulate. Vito was on his knees, taking pictures. Steinberg could hear the repetitious clicking and the electronic advance on Messato's camera.

"Go away," Carolyn hissed. It was not her voice but sounded like the voice Steinberg had heard that day on the third floor.

Steinberg was too awestruck to respond. He felt as if he couldn't move, as though his legs were made of lead and his arms too heavy to lift. Somewhere in the back of his mind, he could hear another voice. It finally registered; it was Vito—tugging at him, pulling him, urging him to leave.

It was impossible for him to turn away. As he would later assess, it was one of the most unbelievable things he had ever witnessed, but he would say he felt compelled to watch it.

Carolyn Messato was undergoing yet another transformation. Her face contorted into a hideous mask composed of a sickly white, bubbling substance that appeared to be melting right in front of Steinberg's horrified eyes. She opened the disfigured slit that had served as her mouth, and a vile, greenish slime erupted, spewing out of her like hot lava flowing from a volcano.

Finally, Steinberg turned away, and he heard a hideous yet fiendishly triumphant laugh. It sounded alternately like a woman and then a child. He dropped to his knees and closed his eyes; when the laughter ceased, he opened them again.

Carolyn Messato was standing over him, staring down at him. She was drained of color and was trembling. Except for the fact that her clothing was drenched with sweat, she looked much the same as she had when the three of them entered the house.

"Grab her," Vito shouted, "before she collapses. It's all over."

Steinberg followed the Messatos back to their apartment in Queens. He replayed the mind-bending sequence of events over and over in his mind as he drove.

Vito had carefully led his wife back to the van and arranged it so she could lie down after her exhausting encounter. Then he went about the process of repacking their gear. Before they left, he talked Steinberg into taking a quick look through the house. To his astonishment, there was no sign of fire, no smoke and no visible changes in the house from when they had entered. Steinberg would tell John Kelly he was astonished. He had seen the flames, felt their heat, choked on the smoke, heard the explosion, saw the brilliant flash of light—yet when he toured the house there was nothing to indicate that any of it had ever happened. He had questions, hundreds of them. What had he been witness to? What had happened? How had Carolyn Messato survive? But Vito Messato would answer none of them.

"We'll talk when we get Carolyn back to the apartment," Vito said as he climbed behind the wheel of his van. Steinberg repeatedly wondered, during the drive back to Queens, how anyone could explain what they had just been through.

It was going on seven o'clock by the time Vito was satisfied that his wife was resting comfortably. It took over four hours for Carolyn's heartbeat to stabilize. Convinced that his wife was out of danger, Vito came back into the room, fixed them each a drink and sat down next to the fireplace. Vito admitted that he was always unnerved by these experiences. He also admitted it was the most violent encounter he had been part of.

"I've heard about that place for years," he said. "I even attended a meeting three years ago when some professor from the Saint Alban Society read his paper on it. Carolyn and I always said that if we ever were given the opportunity to look around over there, we'd jump at it. That's why we were so eager to work with you when Vincent called us."

"Tell me this, Vito. I've been in that old house

twice now, and both times it's been pretty harrowing. How is it that those two boys can go in and out of there without experiencing some of the same things?"

Vito Messato shook his head. "You never know about these things, Lieutenant. No two of them are alike, it seems. Oh, sometimes there is a similarity, but they're never exactly the same. There was a case out on the island several years ago where something went around unscrewing caps on bottles, knocking things over, pictures off the wall, that sort of thing. The family had a parapsychologist from Duke University come in to investigate. Not one thing happened in the two weeks he observed the place. The day he left it started all over again. Eventually it was written off as an authenticated poltergeist experience."

"But we're not dealing with poltergeists here, are we?" Steinberg was amazed at how quickly he was picking up and using Messato's terminology."

Vito shook his head. "Carolyn is the expert. All I do is record the data. But in this case, I'll have to admit that I'm certain we're dealing with something more than poltergeists. I've never seen poltergeists get that violent."

"There's something I need to tell you. This episode didn't turn out anything like I expected. For some reason, I had the impression you and your wife would make a couple of trips through the house, walk out and explain what was going on in there."

Vito laughed for the first time since their encounter. "Actually, Lieutenant, today we only scratched the surface. If you want a full-blown analysis of that old place, what we did today amounts to nothing more than a preliminary peek. We'd have to have a contractor go through that house from top to bottom, check the plumbing, the wiring, the vent systems and a whole lot more. A great many of our so-called ghosts can be taken out of a house by simply taking the physical vibrations out of it. Several years ago there was an old house in Ohio that the owners claimed moaned and groaned like someone was up in the attic dying. What they discovered was that the house had been built right on top of an underground river, and at certain times in the year the water flow was such that it set up vibrations in the foundation that sounded like folks moaning."

"What we saw today had nothing to do with vibrations, Vito, and you know it. You ask me what I saw, and I'll tell you I don't know—but I'll tell you that it scared the hell out of me."

"Words like scary won't hack it, Lieutenant. Carolyn and I will have to get our heads together and document exactly what happened out there today."

"How long will that take?"

"As soon as Carolyn feels up to it. In the meantime I'll review the audio tapes and see what we've got on film. A lot will depend on what Carolyn can remember."

* * *

That evening, as Jerome Steinberg drove back to his apartment, he slipped the small voice recorder out of his coat pocket and placed it on the seat beside him. He had ignored Vito Messato's instructions. The recorder had been on throughout the ordeal. He pressed the rewind button, waited for the click and pressed "play." He was rewarded with the sound of hideous laugh, clear and sinister—and then, silence.

... DAY THIRTEEN ...

On Monday morning, October 25th, Alice Chambers awoke with what she described in her journal as "one of my old headaches." As her diary for the previous day indicates, she had spent long hours anguishing over both the recurring dream of the mother with the thing/child and what she referred to in her diary for the first time as her husband's sickness.

That journal entry, written sometime during the course of the night, follows:

> "I awakened in a terrible sweat. The bedclothes were drenched. I wondered if it was possible that I had the flu since I had a high fever. Roy was still sleeping soundly as I left the room to be with my anguish.

"The dreadful dream continues to haunt me and now comes to me in the day as well. Even now in the harsh light of the lamp on my desk, I see all too plainly the image of that horrifying and evil face. I recoil at the sight of its serpentine features.

"How, I pray thee answer, can a child created in the image and likeness of my savior be so incredibly hideous? What must I do to stamp out this profligacy?"

There is evidence from a later, more erratic passage that Alice May turned her thoughts in the early hours of the morning to the hostility Roy felt for his son. On one particular page, there are a number of disjointed and isolated references, often confined to two or three words, which illustrate that concern. The name of Dr. Spielmann appears twice, both times with question marks behind it. The words "conflict" and "hate" appear several times, twice in large, bold letters. There is even the mention of the house at 112 Ocean Avenue. She asks, "Why do I feel attracted to it?"

The reference to Roy Chambers' hostility reveals a new dimension to Alice Chambers' anguish:

"Twice now he has beaten the boy unmercifully. He seems to revel in the boy's suffering. Could it be that he somehow attaches blame to the boy for his wife's death?"

THE NIGHTMARE CONTINUES

AUTHOR'S NOTE #1: MONICA AND ROY CHAMBERS HAD BEEN MARRIED FOR EIGHT YEARS WHEN ELLEN, THEIR DAUGHTER, WAS BORN. SARA WINE CONDUCTED AN INVESTIGATION INTO THE MATTER AND REVEALED THE FOLLOWING TO JOHN KELLY. A TRANSCRIPTION OF A PORTION OF THAT TAPE FOLLOWS:

WINE: "Roy Chambers had attended a two day conference at Montauk and was driving home, west on Highway 27, when he collided head-on with a bread truck. The driver of the bread truck was killed; Chambers suffered massive internal injuries to the lower pelvic area. He was hospitalized for seven weeks and underwent extensive corrective surgery. He didn't work for almost a year.

"Somewhere along in there, during the convalescence period, Chambers was informed that he would be unable to father any more children. I talked to a Dr. Esterline Webster who claims she told Chambers this during one of the twice-a-week therapy sessions he underwent for almost a year after the accident.

"At the time of the accident, Chambers had been having weekly sessions with Monsignor McConnell at Saint Alomar; the subject was the shaky status of Roy and Monica Chambers' marriage. Roy wanted to get a divorce, but McConnell was discouraging it because of the Catholic view on divorce. Apparently, Chambers thought his wife was having an affair."

KELLY: "Was she?"

WINE: "I don't know. But when she turned up pregnant two years later, Chambers was convinced she was on her second or third affair by that time. Throughout all of this, Roy Chambers continued to have his weekly conversations with McConnell. He wanted a divorce based on infidelity."

KELLY: "But McConnell discouraged him?"

WINE: "Yes. Then she got pregnant and had a baby, the one you know as Lester. One year later she committed suicide."

KELLY: "How?"

WINE: "Overdose of barbiturates during the night, while her husband and the two children were asleep in their rooms."

KELLY: "Was there an investigation?"

WINE: "Yes—but not much of one. The police thought it was pretty clear-cut. She left a note, confessing to past indiscretions and pleading for forgiveness."

AUTHOR'S NOTE #2: THERE IS NOTHING IN JOHN KELLY'S FILES TO INDICATE THAT ALICE CHAMBERS KNEW ANYTHING ABOUT THE DETAILS OF MONICA CHAMBERS' DEATH OR HER CONFESSED INDISCRETIONS AT THIS POINT IN TIME. WHETHER OR NOT ROY CHAMBERS EVER DISCUSSED

THE NIGHTMARE CONTINUES

SOME OF THE MORE INTIMATE DETAILS OF HIS PREVIOUS MARRIAGE WITH ALICE MAY IS A MATTER OF CONJECTURE. IT IS CLEAR, HOWEVER, THAT SOMETIME DURING THE NIGHT OF OCTOBER 24-25, ROY CHAMBERS' OBVIOUS HOSTILITY TOWARD LESTER WAS CLEARLY THE CAUSE OF THE WOMAN'S CONCERN.

Jerome Steinberg was having a cup of coffee when the phone rang.

"Lieutenant?" It was Vito Messato.

"How's Carolyn?"

"Outside of the fact that she still seems a bit shook up, she appears to be okay. She was too strung out to go to work today, though. How about you?"

"Stiff, sore, confused, perplexed; give me a couple of seconds and I'll think of some more."

"Did you get anything on your tape?"

Steinberg hesitated. Messato had told him to turn it off. "Matter of fact, I didn't," he finally admitted. Carolyn Messato, he thought to himself, didn't miss much.

"Me neither. Looks like we drew blanks all the way around. I stayed up half the night trying to develop the film we shot. Nothing. Zippo. Every last frame is a bust."

"What about your audio?"

"Garbage. Pure static."

"You don't actually think it's possible all four pieces of equipment malfunctioned, do you?" Steinberg asked.

"Not likely. I think we're on to something."

175

"Meaning?"

Vito hesitated. "Look, Lieutenant, I don't usually do this, but under the circumstances, I'm going to tell you what Carolyn told me before I left for work. None of this is official you realize, but Carolyn believes we're actually dealing with two influences in that old place. She thinks the influences are in conflict."

"Interpret that for me?"

"Carolyn thinks there is an influence that wants us to stay out—and another one that wants to get out. She says she actually got a warning from the first one. She interpreted it as wanting to shield her from the other influence. She says the second one is just plain nasty." Vito laughed when he used the word "nasty."

Steinberg recalls that he wasn't sure how to respond to Vito's input, but before he could, the line went dead. For the next several hours, he tried to call the Messato residence to check on Carolyn and get the phone number of Vito's office. There was no answer at the Messato residence. And, when he attempted to call Vincent Chiraldi, he was informed that Chiraldi would not return until after six that evening.

In the Saint Alomar cafeteria the lunch period was nearly over. Kooch Webster was keeping his voice low.

"So I stopped last night and picked up the teapot and cups. I went over to the house last Saturday after me and Mom got back from the funeral home. I put a bunch of stuff in the old boathouse.''

Lester still had his mouth full of Jello. "How come? You know you can't sell it to old man Silverman anymore."

Kooch leaned back in his chair, disregarding the second bell. "Hey, man, I've got an even better idea."

"Old man Silverman had the only pawnshop in town," Lester reminded him.

Kooch frowned. "You know what the trouble with you is, dinkhead?"

Lester shook his head. "Naw, what?"

"You got no imagination. You look right at somethin' and don't see the possibilities. Me, I'm the kind that sees things. We pawned that stuff with Silverman, right?"

Lester nodded.

"You know what happened to Silverman, don't ya?"

"Somebody killed 'em, I guess."

"What do you mean, 'you guess'? Hell, there was the pictures of the old fart right there on the front page of the paper. He was deader than a doornail. I read it. It said that somebody drove that old tool I pawned right through his heart. And what about the cat? You saw that, didn't ya? The cat was dead, too. He drank from the bowl, and—zap—the bowl got 'em. You know why? Because that drill and that bowl were haunted."

Lester rolled his eyes. "Naw, no way. Yer jerkin' my chain." He didn't tell Kooch that he

wasn't all that anxious to talk about dead people
—or for that matter, dead cats either. Talking
about things like that gave him a queasy feeling
in the pit of his stomach.

"Hey, dumbo, listen to me. Remember that
watch I put in my grandma's purse?"

"What watch?" Lester vaguely remembered
something Kooch had told him about a watch,
but he couldn't remember what.

"Don't ya remember? I found an old watch in
the house. It was broken, but I put it in Grandma
Jacalyn's purse. And you know what? The
dipshit was wearing it the night she was in the
accident."

Lester had forgotten all about it. It didn't
seem very important at the time, and he didn't
understand why Kooch was making such a big
deal out of it now. "So?" he said.

"How come I have to explain everything to
you?" Kooch complained.

Lester shrugged. He guessed it was because
Kooch was smarter than he was. At that particular moment, he couldn't think of any other
reason. "Whatcha gettin' at?"

"I think," Kooch lowered his voice, "that all
that stuff we been takin' out of that old house is
really haunted."

Lester wanted to remind him that the only
thing he had personally taken was a belt and a
bowl. Kooch had taken everything else—and if
the stuff was haunted, which he doubted, that
was Kooch's problem. "Awwww," he drawled,

"that stuff ain't haunted. You don't really believe that crap, do you?"

"I sure do. All you gotta do is think about it. First we sell the stuff to Silverman, and bingo, he gets croaked. Then I slip the watch in grandma's purse, and she gets run over by a train. What's that tell ya?"

Lester wasn't quite sure what it did tell him. His only regret was the belt; he wished he had never seen it. His father had used it on him twice. "I think that stuff Moe is sellin' ya is gettin' to ya, that's what I think."

"You got a better explanation for them dyin'?"

Lester had to think. He had heard of haunted houses, haunted castles and haunted buildings like opera houses and churches—but he had never heard of haunted tools, dishes and watches. "Awwww," he drawled again.

"I can prove it," Kooch challenged.

"How?"

"By givin' somethin' to somebody else and seein' what happens to 'em."

"Like who?"

"What's wrong with givin' somethin' to old lady Camino?"

"But you don't even like her. How come you're gonna give her somethin'?"

"Because, dink, she's the one that got us in all this trouble in the first place. When you stop to think about it, all these detentions are her fault. If she hadn't squealed on us, we'd never have gone into that old house in the first place."

Lester knew he was a slow thinker, but he was confused. He was having trouble tying their troubles with Monsignor McConnell and Sister Bertha to Silverman, Kooch's grandmother, and now Mrs. Camino.

"See, what I'm gonna do is give that teapot to Mrs. Camino, and if somethin' happens to her, we'll know that stuff is haunted. Right?"

"Awwww, you'd have to prove it to me." Lester was feeling unusually brave. He seldom talked back to Kooch. Normally he believed what Kooch told him and didn't question him.

"You'll see," Kooch said.

As far as Lester was concerned, he couldn't have cared less whether Kooch gave the teapot to Mrs. Camino or not; he had his own problems to worry about. Besides, he was convinced Kooch was baiting him with all this talk about the things he had stolen being haunted. "Give it to her," he said. "Who cares?"

At that very moment, Lester felt a hand clamp down on his shoulder. He looked up into the cold, dispassionate eyes of Sister Bertha.

"Well, Lester, I see you're late for class again. The cafeteria closed ten minutes ago."

Later that afternoon, Lester vowed that if Kooch Webster turned out to be right and the items he was taking from the house on Ocean Avenue really were haunted, he wanted one to give to Sister Bertha.

At 9:07 Steinberg shoveled the day's paperwork back into his briefcase and turned on the television to watch Monday Night Football. The game had been temporarily interrupted because of an injury on the field. He had just sat down in his easy chair when the phone rang. It was Father Vincent Chiraldi.

"Jerry," the priest asked, "have you talked to Vito Messato?"

"Early this morning. We got cut off, and I haven't been able to get in touch with him since."

"Carolyn is in Sacred Heart Hospital," Chiraldi interrupted. "I'm on my way over to see her. I wonder if you want to tag along."

"Is it serious?"

"I think so. Vito is pretty shook up. Carolyn is in the intensive care unit."

By the time the two men arrived at Sacred Heart Hospital, Steinberg had filled Chiraldi in on the happenings of the previous day at the house on Ocean Avenue. The priest listened, commenting only after Steinberg mentioned that neither the audio tapes nor the film had given them anything to go on.

"I guess I'm not surprised," Chiraldi admitted. "I've done some checking into the last episode out there. A couple of fairly reputable sources assure me that it wasn't a fraud."

Steinberg would mention this particular conversation to Kelly almost as an afterthought, telling John that he was amazed at the awareness of the house throughout the parapsychological network.

On the hospital's third floor, west wing, the two men were ushered into an isolated IC unit where a distraught Vito Messato and a nurse kept their eyes fixed on a bank of electronic monitors. After Vito and the priest embraced, Chiraldi went to the woman's bedside. He laid his hands on hers and closed his eyes in prayer.

Vito took Steinberg by the arm and steered him back into the lighted corridor. "Did you get a look at her?" Vito asked.

Steinberg hadn't. "What happened?"

Vito, red-eyed and worried, dropped into a nearby chair. He fumbled for a cigarette, lit it, took a deep drag and then exhaled. "Jesus, Jerry, I don't know what happened. She called me at work. It was around noon. She said she felt terrible. That isn't like her; she never calls me at work or complains. Even over the phone I could hear her gasping for breath. I raced home and found her in the bathtub. It was full of scalding water. She was frantic."

"Scalding water?" Steinberg repeated.

"I don't know what was going on in her head. She said it was all over her. I couldn't see anything. When I got her out of the tub, she had third degree burns over her entire body. Then I called the emergency unit."

Steinberg went back into the IC unit and headed straight for the woman's bedside. Carolyn Messato's face had been burned beyond recognition. Just beneath the surface of the skin was a network of bloated, pulsating blood vessels, as if the life-sustaining fluid was boiling.

Plastic tubes had been inserted into what was left of her nose and mouth.

Steinberg recoiled, looked away and turned back to look at her again. Carolyn was staring at him with unseeing eyes. He stepped away, tried to catch his breath and looked at the nurse. She was shaking her head. Chiraldi had donned his scapular and laid a rosary on the strips of gauze covering the charred remains of the woman's hands. The priest's eyes were closed and his lips formed a stream of silent prayer.

Steinberg continued to look at the nurse, his eyes asking the question. The woman diverted her attention from the monitors just long enough to form the words, "Last rites."

At 11:46 P.M., on October 25th, Jerome Steinberg was informed of Carolyn Messato's passing.

Father Vincent Chiraldi put his hands on the officer's shoulder. "She passed from this life just a few moments ago," the priest said—and then he began to weep.

. . . DAY FOURTEEN . . .

It was 7:00 A.M., Tuesday, October 26th. Lt. Jerome Steinberg trudged across the parking lot behind the police station after reporting the distressing and untimely death of Carolyn Messato to Stephen Carr.

Steinberg was weary. He had been up for over 24 hours. On his way home, he purchased a morning paper and quickly scanned the sports pages while he had breakfast at a small diner on Dunheim Avenue. He intended to grab a quick shower, an hour's worth of sleep, and then talk to both Charla Webster and Alice Chambers about the footprints in the mud behind the house on Ocean Avenue. Steinberg was convinced that one or both of the boys had returned

184

to the house and stolen more items. While the theft of itself was minor, he was more concerned about the bizarre happenings that occurred during the Messato investigation. Steinberg intended to warn the two mothers that the boys were not safe.

Steinberg took his shower and lay down across the bed. He did not warn Charla Webster or Alice Chambers about the danger to their sons. He slept through the day and into the small hours of the morning.

That same morning, after Charla Webster sent her son off to school following the three day mourning period, she began to wander aimlessly through the empty house. In the space of the last 12 months, the woman had lost her mother, a brother and a favorite uncle. During that same period, she had finalized her divorce and moved to Amityville to be near her mother. Now her mother was dead, and with the exception of her son, Donald, she was alone.

Rambling aimlessly from room to room, mentally inventorying her life, she eventually came to her son's room on the second floor. Once again, she discovered a curious assortment of items she would not have expected to find. There was a small, digital clock radio with a knob missing, a silver cigarette lighter and a bone china tea service. The latter was exquisite, elaborately decorated with gold leaf and hand-painted tea roses. Charla knew very little about fine porcelain, but she did recognize the quality of the pieces sitting on her son's dresser. She made a mental note to ask him about it.

Gerald Harrison, the manager of the Rockmeyer Funeral Home, was alone in his office. He had come in early that morning for the express purpose of cleaning up a backlog of paperwork that had accumulated over the past couple of days. The establishment had been unusually busy for the past several weeks, and he had decided to devote the entire day to administrative matters.

He removed the Jacalyn Cordes file from his briefcase and was appalled to discover that none of the documentation was complete. There was no record of services performed, no itemizing of expenses, and the copy of the death certificate had not been filled out. The paperwork relative to the casket purchase by Charla Webster was missing, and the embalming agreement was unsigned.

Disgusted with what he considered to be the inefficiencies of his staff, he reproached his secretary, Linda Royerton, for her lack of attention to details. He instructed her to complete the paperwork and returned to his office to call the courthouse to apologize for the delay. State law required that all paperwork persuant to a client's burial be forwarded in 72 hours.

That evening Gerald Harrison told his wife about the Cordes situation in great detail, complaining that he had never had a set of circumstances where so many things had gone wrong. Four years later, in his one and only interview with John Myron Kelly, Harrison was unwilling to discuss many of the details of the Cordes funeral. What information John Kelly was able to obtain came from Linda Royerton and Mrs. Harrison. Gerald Harrison died two months after his meeting with John Kelly of a heart attack.

At 3257 Oak Street, Alice Chambers agreed to a 10:30 A.M. meeting with Dr. Crispman and Dr. Spielmann the following morning. Following that call, she recorded that she felt a strong compulsion to spend time with her journal. She had devoted the early part of the day to mundane household chores, and as the hours wore on, the desire to spend time with her thoughts intensified.

The first entries on this date consist mostly of Alice Chambers' feelings about the Chambers children, her husband, and what she referred to as her lot in life. On the second page dated the 26th, she again turned her thoughts to the recurring dream or vision. She described it in exacting detail, dwelling on the meaning of the woman carrying the child/thing.

Although she does not elaborate on when or why the idea first occurred to her, it is apparent from one particularly convoluted and troubled passage that she had been thinking about going into the house on Ocean Avenue. The painful process of rationalization leading up to her decision is apparent. Why she chose to do it on this particular day is unknown. The entry, however, is paintaking in it's detail:

"Although the depressing grayness of the early hours gave way to a brash and windy autumn afternoon bathed in full sunlight, the house itself maintained an aura of brooding.

"As I approached the house, I became more and more aware of the sense of the sinister and the threatening. Was it my imagination, or was it truly a place that gave sanctuary to evil?

"In the driveway, a chill wind swirled about me, and I felt the distressing awareness of my aloneness. Fear was clinging tenaciously to me, and I shuddered my first prayer.

"It took a great deal more strength than I had imagined just to climb those steps and peer beyond the darkened windows. The soulless objects that I knew dwelled therein gave the interior an aura of foreboding.

"I tried the door; it opened easily. I was surprised that it was not locked. Was it an invitation? After entering those awful confines, I wondered if I possessed either the strength and the faith to continue. Why, I asked myself, would she be in this place? Yet I knew I would find her—her and that frightful child/thing. Perhaps it was not her choice. Perhaps it was ordained.

"There were sounds of great suffering and

sadness, and there was the overpowering aroma of perfume. It was sickeningly sweet, designed more, I think, to cover up the smell of something unpleasant rather than to please the senses.

"I stood trembling at the base of the stairs leading to the upper level, knowing full well that she would soon appear. I do not know how I knew that she would be in this place of unspeakable coldness and overwhelming sadness.

"Before she appeared, I knew that I would have to undergo a test, that there would be a sequence of things to be endured. I had every intention of fortifying myself with silent prayer, but I could not think of the words to any prayer. My thoughts became chaotic and confused. There was a brash chill and then a cacophony of shrill and discordant sounds. The house groaned. The floors creaked. The smell of the perfume intensified. I waited, and my heart was filled with fear.

"Suddenly she appeared. In her arms she held the swaddled creature. She was standing on the landing at the top of the stairs. Slowly, methodically, but without malice, she began to descend the stairs. I trembled as she began to peel away the wraps, and when she did, I realized the creature was more hideous than ever.

"Its misshapen head was inclined toward me. Its forked tongue darted in and out of its cruel mouth like a great, evil serpent. It *hissed and gave off a foul odor that overpowered even the pungent smell of the perfume.*

"Terror filled my heart. I was looking upon the face of evil incarnate.

" 'Yes,' she said. 'It is mine, of my own flesh and blood. Now you know. Now you must go away.'

"I recoiled.

"The child/thing leaped from her arms and disgorged itself from the filthy rags that encased it. It slithered and clawed at me, making terrifying noises.

"I reached out for it. I would embrace it—and in doing so, submit my soul.

" 'No,' the woman screamed. 'Go!'

"I fled from the house in terror."

Sometime during the dark hours that followed, Alice May made her final entry of the day. In the following brief description, she interprets her encounter:

"I know now what I have been witness to. I have looked into the face of the source of all evil. It is her burden. Our God has cast it upon her. The woman is the consummate source of all that is corrupt and depraved— and the thing/child is the fruit of her evil womb, the darkest of angels.

... DAY FIFTEEN ...

On the morning of Wednesday, October 27th,
Monsignor McConnell, following morning
Mass, stood at the entrance to the Saint Alomar
Academy main corridor to greet the students. It
was the first time he had done so in ten days. He
glowered at both Donald Webster and Lester
Chambers as they passed him. Despite his prolonged fast, the Monsignor had kept abreast of
activities at the school. Sister Bertha's report on
her meeting with Roy and Alice Chambers had
been duly noted.

At about the same time, Jerome Steinberg
awoke with the groggy, sluggish feeling of a man
who has had too much of the wrong kind of
sleep. His first act of the day was a long steaming
shower that he hoped would clear away the

cobwebs. He followed that with a quick breakfast and a call to Stephen Carr to arrange a midmorning meeting.

Later that morning, Alice Chambers sat down at a conference table across from Dr. Spielmann and Dr. Crispman.

"I realize that we have asked you here on short notice, Mrs. Chambers, but when Dr. Spielmann informed me that he would be in Europe the next three weeks, I thought it best to have this meeting before he left."

Alice was uncomfortable in such a setting, admitting in her journal that she was concerned and frightened. Was Lester terribly ill? Did the spreading black stain portend some terrible, debilitating disease? She feared the worst. The doctor had been vague over the telephone.

Crispman cleared his throat. "When you first brought Lester's problem to my attention, I believed that Lester had contracted a rare form of skin cancer. But, as you recall, I was not very confident with my diagnosis, and that's why I asked you to see Dr. Spielmann. Well, it's a good thing we did. Dr. Spielmann has ruled out any form of melanoma."

As Alice breathed a sigh of relief, Spielmann spoke up. "That's the good news, Mrs. Chambers. The bad news is we don't have a fix on your son's problem yet. That's why we wanted to talk to you. The tissue samples we took from Lester have undergone extensive evaluation, and, as of this moment, we have to report that we can find no pathological explanation for the spreading discoloration. However, when I called Dr. Crispman to discuss the matter with him, he indicated that Lester has experienced difficulties in the past."

Alice continued to stare at the two men.

"You are aware, of course, that we have treated Lester for hives and rashes many times in the past, usually after he has undergone a rather stressful experience," Crispman said.

Alice shook her head. "No, I wasn't aware of it," she admitted.

"What Dr. Crispman is saying, Mrs. Chambers, is that after my conversations with him I felt that we should explore Lester's medical history in detail. Based on what Dr. Crispman has told me, I'm lead to believe there is a possibility your son is simply manifesting prior problems in a new and somewhat more dramatic light."

"I—I don't understand what you're talking about."

The two men looked at each other, and Spielmann shifted in his chair.

"Are you not aware that that Lester suffers from some deeply rooted pysochological and emotional problems, Mrs. Chambers?" Crispman seemed surprised that the woman's husband had not discussed the matter with her.

Alice shook her head.

Crispman hesitated. He looked uneasy with what he was about to reveal. "Monica Chambers committed suicide one year after Lester's birth." His voice was unemotional. "Your husband was very distraught, and the only solution to the problem appeared to be long-term psychological therapy. In the final analysis, I'm afraid that therapy wasn't quite as effective as we hoped it would be. Indications are that Roy Chambers did then and still does see Lester as the catalyst that ultimately forced Monica Chambers to take her own life."

"But why?"

"Because your husband knows that Lester is not his son."

Alice was too stunned to speak. "I—I didn't know about Mrs. Chambers," she stammered.

"This is most unfortunate," Crispman said. "I naturally assumed that you and your husband would have discussed this matter."

Spielmann leaned forward, nervously rotating his glasses back and forth between his large hands. "Dr. Crispman tells me that Lester is a very sensitive boy who tries very hard to please everyone. If that is the case, we have a psychological profile which, when combined with other factors in his background and coupled with the trauma of his early years, could cause a self-induced manifestation of his feelings of guilt."

"Has Lester been in some sort of trouble lately?" Crispman pressed.

"He has been doing very poorly at school."

"Is he under a great deal of pressure?" Spielmann continued.

Alice May balked. "His—his father has severely reprimanded him for a recent incident."

"May I inquire what?"

"He—he stole some things from a deserted house."

Crispman leaned back in his chair and looked at Spielmann. "Under the circumstances, Alice, I'm going to share some information with you that I believe you need to know. However, our conversation must be held in the strictest confidence. Do you understand?"

Alice nodded.

"For a number of years prior to his wife's death, Roy Chambers sought counsel from Monsignor McConnell regarding his marriage. I will say only this much. At the time of Monica Chambers' death, there was a great deal of stress in the relationship, primarily because of the baby Roy Chambers knew he had not fathered. I would advise you to talk to Monsignor McConnell. I believe you need to have a better understanding of the conditions that preceded you. McConnell, more than anyone else, can help you get a handle on the relationship between Lester and your husband."

When Alice started to protest, Spielmann held up his hand. "I don't think you understand the full impact of what we are telling you, Mrs. Chambers. When Dr. Crispman contacted Saint Alomar two days ago, he was informed that Lester is again exhibiting signs of . . . if not abuse, overly severe parental punishment. It has happened before. But now, under New York state law, school officials must report cases of suspected child abuse."

Tears formed in Alice's eyes, and the words blurted out. "He used a belt on Lester. It was a belt that Lester stole."

Spielmann's face was implacable. "Severe punishment for an eleven-year-old," he said flatly.

"Especially an overly sensitive boy that worships his father," Crispman added.

Spielmann stood up and began to pace back and forth. "I think we will eventually learn that your stepson's problem is a manifestation of his guilt feelings over displeasing his father in the only way he knows how—a self-induced and to him wholly acceptable way of acknowledging his imperfection and indiscretion. In other words, he wants his father to know he is sorry, and the skin blemish is a kind of obvious sackcloth he can wear like the sinner he believes himself to be."

There was a long silence before Alice May asked, "Will it go away?"

Spielmann sighed. "It could, but not until Lester is able to eliminate his conflict and convince himself that he is secure in his father's love."

"Is there anything I can do to help?"

"You can talk to Monsignor McConnell. That much is imperative."

"Thank you," Alice said. She left the meeting without telling the two men about the episode with Lester's jacket. Neither did she tell them about Roy Chambers' increasingly morose behavior.

Later that day, after Alice Chambers returned home from her meeting with the two doctors, Charla Webster called her to make arrangements for Donald to come home with Lester after school. She informed Alice that she had to go into the city and would not return home until later that evening when she expected to pick up her son around 9:00 P.M.

Charla did not pick up her son until shortly after 11:00 P.M. She had been drinking heavily, and Alice was hesitant to let the woman drive, even though it was only a few blocks.

At about the same time that Charla Webster was picking up her son at the Chambers' house, Father Vincent Chiraldi received a phone call from a man who identified himself as Leonard Leland. Mr. Leland was the superintendent of the apartment house in Queens where Vito and Carolyn Messato lived. He informed Father Chiraldi that there had been a tragedy.

"Mr. Messato has committed suicide. I found a note on the mirror in the bathroom where he did it. The note said to call you. The police are here, and they said what with you being a priest and all, it was all right."

. . . DAY SIXTEEN . . .

Virginia Heart escorted Lt. Steinberg to the Monsignor's study on the second floor, took his coat and excused herself, closing the door behind her. It was a few minutes after ten o'clock, Thursday morning, October 28th.

Another day had dawned gray and windy, and by the time Steinberg arrived at the austere Saint Alomar rectory, a steady and monotonous drizzle had set in. Alone in the room while he waited for the Monsignor, he walked over to the gas fireplace to warm his hands.

When David McConnell entered the room a few minutes later, Steinberg was taken aback by the man's altered appearance. The priest's face was drawn and haggard. His cassock fit him poorly, and the scarlet sash hung loosely around his waist.

"Ahh, Lt. Steinberg, how nice to see you again. Are you here because you have some news about Father Bellini?"

"I'm afraid not, sir."

McConnell shook his head and pursed his thin lips. He looked disappointed. Steinberg wondered if he knew anything about Bellini's rumored relationship with the mysterious and missing Judith Brewer. It was an aspect of the Bellini case that Steinberg had decided not to bring up unless McConnell mentioned it.

The two men were still exchanging pleasantries when Mrs. Heart knocked discreetly. She entered, served tea and departed without saying a word. Steinberg had just picked up his cup when McConnell cleared his throat.

"Why is it I get the feeling, Lieutenant, that your visit relates to something totally unexpected? You strike me as the kind of man who breaks concrete with a tapping action instead of brute strength."

Steinberg laughed. "Isn't that the best way to go about it? On the other hand, maybe you have that feeling because you're right on target. We're still looking into Father Bellini's disappearance all right, but I'm sorry to say we haven't made much headway. On the other hand, there are a couple of other, perhaps related, matters on my mind as well."

McConnell arched his thin gray eyebrows. He

had taken a seat directly across from Steinberg, and the oversized wing chair completely enfolded him. Steinberg realized that by sitting in the chair, McConnell had minimized the significant difference in their sizes.

"Am I supposed to ask what other matters, Lieutenant?"

Steinberg hesitated. "What I'm about to tell you, sir, may test the limits of my credibility, but I believe you may be one of the few people who can shed some light on all of this."

"Try me, Lieutenant." Steinberg could tell that the man was flattered. "I'm at your service."

Steinberg would later say that he was relieved to see how easy it was to guide McConnell through the convoluted maze of events since Bellini's disappearance. He covered the bizarre circumstances surrounding the Silverman murder, touched briefly on the untimely death of Jacalyn Cordes, and tied the two seemingly unrelated incidents to the fact that Bellini was missing. He then went into more detail as he recounted the events of the past 72 hours and the unfortunate deaths of both Carolyn and Vito Messato.

McConnell's reaction caught him off guard. The priest stared stoically back at him, his pasty face fixed in an indifferent frown.

"That's all very interesting, Lieutenant, but I fail to see why you think I would be interested in this rather unfortunate series of events. I am interested in what you learn about Father

Bellini—not some supposedly haunted house. Don't tell me you think all of this somehow relates to Saint Alomar."

"On the contrary, Monsignor. All I've given you so far is the prologue, a little background material. Now come the questions."

McConnell squinted his eyes. He was perceptibly less affable than he had been at the outset. "Proceed if you must, Lieutenant."

"I understand you have been at Saint Alomar for the past fifteen years, sir. If that's the case, you were here when they had all the notoriety about the house in Amityville, the one on Ocean Avenue."

"Need I remind the Lieutenant that Saint Alomar is located in Glencoe, not Amityville. I had no interest in the media circus created by the former owner of that house, what with his ghosts and other ludicrous claims. No one, I repeat, no one at Saint Alomar was even remotely associated with that debacle."

"I wasn't implying that anyone was, sir. I was simply leading up to this question. Did you know Father Mancuso, and if you did, did you ever talk to him about his experience?"

McConnell was visibly agitated. Tiny beads of sweat had formed on his forehead, and he shifted in his chair. "First of all, Lieutenant, I did not know Father Mancuso. Secondly, I would not have discussed that ridiculous matter with him if I had. The alleged involvement of a Roman Catholic priest in such a matter is beyond my comprehension. The entire affair was a hoax, irrational people with overly active imaginations trying to convince the all-too-gullible public of the existence of evil spirits. It was a blatant attempt on the part of unfortunate people to capitalize on the fears and superstitions of others even less fortunate."

"Is that all you have to say on the matter?"

"Not quite, Lieutenant. I have a statement to make. The Holy Mother Church has far more important matters to deal with than hobgoblins and spooks, especially those conjured up by money-grubbing charlatans."

McConnell stood up, and when that didn't seem to relieve his tension, he began rocking back and forth on his heels.

"Suppose I told you that we have reason to believe that some of your students may be involved in this most recent series of events?"

McConnell stopped. "That, Lieutenant, is preposterous."

"I'm afraid not. One, or quite possibly two of them, has repeatedly been stealing from the house in question."

"I suppose you have proof?" McConnell challenged.

"No sir, not the kind that would stand up in court, and I can't give you specifics because the investigation is still underway. I'm sure you are aware that it's no small matter to bring charges against minors. However, if it can be proven that two Saint Alomar students were stealing items on their way to and from school, you and your staff could unwittingly receive some very unfavorable publicity."

"Is that a threat, Lieutenant?"

"Not at all, Monsignor."

"Then I've heard quite enough, Lieutenant. Are you through?"

Steinberg stood up. When he did, he towered over the little man. "Tell me, Monsignor, what's with you? Is it that you don't believe what people say happened in that old house, or could it be that you're afraid there is some truth to it?"

McConnell's cheeks were suddenly tinged with pink. "Your comments border on impertinence, Lieutenant." The priest walked to the door and opened it. "Now, sir, if you will be so kind as to leave, I have other more important matters to attend to than stand here and listen to false charges and outlandish accusations."

Steinberg was halfway through the door when he stopped. "I'll let you know if anything turns up on Father Bellini."

"Don't bother, Lieutenant. If you persist, I will be forced to report your rude behavior and obvious disrespect for a spokesman of the Church to your superiors. And that, Lieutenant, would not look good on your record."

Steinberg leaned forward and lowered his voice. "You do that, Monsignor, and I'll tell them you refused to cooperate with the police in our investigation into the disappearance of Father Bellini."

Steinberg heard the door slam behind him as

he descended the stairs to the first floor. On a hunch, he meandered down the hall to the rectory kitchen. Virginia Heart was standing at the sink, looking out over the brown-gray stretch of winter lawn.

"Thank you for all your help, Mrs. Heart," Steinberg said. The woman turned away from the window and smiled at him. "Take care of Monsignor McConnell; he's quite a guy."

"Had a good talk, did you?" The woman smiled. "The Monsignor is a treasure, isn't he?"

"Know who he reminds me of?"

The woman shook her head.

"He reminds me of Father Mancuso."

Virginia Heart laughed. "Oh, no way, they're entirely different. No comparison."

"Don't tell me you know Father Mancuso, too?"

"Well, of course, I do. I used to call him Father M when he lived around here. He was over here all the time. He used to spend half his time peeking in my refrigerator. He and the Monsignor were very good friends. They played chess and had those long discussions—always arguing, those two."

"Well, if you see him," Steinberg said, grinning, "tell him his old buddy down at the Suffolk County police department said hi."

"Oh, I haven't seen Father M in years, but if I do I'll certainly tell him."

On the steps of the Saint Alomar rectory, Steinberg pulled out his day log and made a brief note. "McConnell lied about knowing

Mancuso. Ask Carr what he knows about Mc-Connell."

As the result of Sister Bertha's decree, Lester was banned from riding the Saint Alomar school bus. Kooch, on his first day back at school, had received a similar fate but hadn't told his mother. As a result, Alice Chambers picked up the two boys at the close of the school day. Exhibiting surprisingly good manners to Mrs. Chambers, Kooch excused himself just long enough to run over to Mrs. Camino's school bus before it departed.

"My mom says I should apologize for being so much trouble. She said I should give you this." He thrust a clumsily wrapped package at the woman. "It ain't much, but it's pretty. I bought it with my own money at a garage sale."

The astonished wife of Charley Camino was barely able to mutter a thank you before the boy darted away.

In a phone conversation later that evening with Charla Webster, after the woman had picked up her son at the Chambers house, Mrs. Charles Camino thanked Donald's mother for her thoughtfulness. The teapot, she said, was lovely.

Charla had no idea who the woman was or what she was talking about. Nor did she care. She had been drinking, and the conversation was little more than a blur.

. . . DAY SEVENTEEN . . .

"Look, Mrs. Webster, there's every indication your son has gone back into that house on Ocean Avenue to steal things." Steinberg's voice was edgy.

Charla Webster started to protest, sighed, got up and walked to the window. She had had a very long day and endured it all with a hangover from the previous night's bout of drinking. Her company was involved in a protracted legal battle with a competitor over patent infringements, and she had suffered through several long and tedious meetings during the course of the day. She was tired and irritable. That, coupled with Steinberg's unexpected visit with more bad news about her son, only compounded her problems.

"Excuse me, Lieutenant," she said, "I was drawing a bath when you knocked, and I need to turn the water off." Charla left the room for several minutes, and when she returned she was wearing a terrycloth bathrobe. She was also carrying a drink.

"I'd offer you something, Lieutenant, but I know you're on duty."

Steinberg smiled and slipped his day log out of his shirt pocket. "Last Sunday, Mrs. Webster, we discovered that additional items had been removed from the house on Ocean Avenue and stored in the old boathouse at the back of the property."

"And you're accusing Donald?"

"He's done it before," Steinberg reminded her. "I was there early enough in the day that I figure whoever stashed those items in the boathouse must have done it the day before."

"Then that lets Donald out, Lieutenant. My son was at the funeral home with me last Saturday, and when we returned home, our family conducted a wake for my mother. We came home late in the afternoon, and I can vouch for the fact that my son spent the rest of the day in the house with me and his two aunts. And just for the record, Lt. Steinberg, I have two very reputable people that can corroborate my story."

AUTHOR'S NOTE: AT A LATER DATE, CHÄRLA WEBSTER ADMITTED TO HER AUNT, CLARA MORRISON, THAT WHEN STEINBERG MADE

HIS ACCUSATIONS, SHE HAD A VIVID REC-
OLLECTION OF THE NIGHT HER MOTHER
SCOLDED DONALD FOR BREAKING INTO
THE POSTED HOUSE. SHE WOULD ALSO AD-
MIT THAT SHE HAD FORGOTTEN ALL ABOUT
THE FACT THAT DONALD HAD ASKED HER
PERMISSION TO GO FOR A WALK THAT EVE-
NING. SHE COULD NOT RECALL HOW LONG
HER SON WAS GONE.

"I was wondering if you would have any
objection to me talking to your son, Mrs. Webster?"

"Is it absolutely necessary, Lieutenant? Do I
need to remind you that Donald has been
through a very difficult period, losing his grandmother and all?"

Steinberg was growing impatient. "That
house is posted, Mrs. Webster. There are 'no
trespassing' signs posted everywhere. The county posted it because it is a crime scene. If we
prove that your son is actually the one stealing
items from that house, any number of charges
could be brought against him—and the least of
those is theft. I don't think you realize the
seriousness of the matter, Mrs. Webster."

"Don't patronize me, Lieutenant. I am a
member of the New York Bar Association."

Steinberg barged ahead. "Two weeks ago,
Father Vincent Bellini's car was found abandoned in the driveway of the house at 112 Ocean
Avenue. Father Bellini is still missing, and we
have reason to suspect foul play. Technically,

that address is now the site of an ongoing investigation. If your son is caught stealing from that house, he could very well be implicated in something far worse than petty theft or breaking and entering."

"Bellini?" Charla repeated. "Father Bellini from Saint Alomar?"

Steinberg nodded. He was anxious to avoid talking about the Bellini investigation, but he had to ask, "Did you know him?"

"Only by name."

"Last week I talked to Mrs. Chambers, Lester's mother, about her son's role in this matter. In essence, I gave her the same warning."

"If Donald has been doing something wrong," Charla said, "then I can assure you it's because that Chambers boy put him up to it."

"I'm not here to bring charges against your son, Mrs. Webster. I'm here to warn you—and to tell you that it is very important for you to keep your son away from that house. If he persists in going back there, I'll see that charges are brought against him if for no other reason than to protect him."

Charla was too weary to argue and far too weary to spar with the officer. She knew Steinberg was right. Somewhere, Donald, like everything else in her life, had gone wrong. For a moment she considered letting the officer talk to her son—maybe, just maybe, he could get through to the boy. Then she decided against it. "You . . . you could talk to him if he was here," she said.

"He's out?"

"With friends," she lied. "He's at the movies. I'll talk to him when he comes home."

Steinberg stood up, thanked the woman and started for the door. "It's for his own good, believe me," he said as an afterthought.

By the time Steinberg had backed out of her driveway, Charla had checked on her son and found him sprawled across his bed with his stereo headset on. Then she went on to take her long-awaited bath.

AUTHOR'S NOTE #1: IN AN INTERVIEW WITH CLARA MORRISON, MONTHS AFTER THE ATTENDENT PUBLICITY TO WHAT CAME TO BE KNOWN AS "THE SECOND AMITYVILLE INCIDENT" DIED DOWN, THE WOMAN ADMITTED THAT HER NIECE KNEW, LONG BEFORE STEINBERG'S VISIT, THAT DONALD WAS OUT OF CONTROL. THE REAL PROBLEM, HOWEVER, WAS THAT CHARLA WEBSTER DID NOT KNOW WHAT TO DO ABOUT IT.

AUTHOR'S NOTE #2: WHILE THERE IS NOTHING IN THE KELLY FILE TO INDICATE WHEN AND HOW THE DECISION WAS MADE, IT IS APPARENT THAT DONALD, HAVING ALREADY GIVEN A PRESENT TO MRS. CHARLES CAMINO TO PROVE TO LESTER THAT ITEMS TAKEN FROM THE HOUSE HAD EVIL POWERS, ALSO SELECTED A GIFT FOR SISTER BERTHA. THAT GIFT WAS A SILVER

CANDELABRA, ALSO STOLEN FROM THE HOUSE ON OCEAN AVENUE.

At the close of the day, Alice Chambers could claim that she had accomplished everything on her agenda. Like every other Friday, she had gone to the market, been to confession, and in general had things laid out for the weekend. Roy Chambers, as was his custom, bowled and had not as yet returned home when Alice May retired to her button room.

The entry for Friday, October 29th, would indicate that she was contemplating a second visit to the house on Ocean Avenue. In her journal she wrote:

"It is my obligation, my destiny, to accept this awful burden. I must correct that which is wrongful and evil. I must go back and help her."

At the same time that Alice Chambers recorded her troubled thoughts in her journal, across town in the Fielding Addition, Mr. and Mrs. Charles Camino were hosting the monthly meeting of the Saint Alomar Lay Guidance Committee. In addition to Charles Camino and his wife, Ruby, there were three other people present: Monsignor David McConnell, Mr. George Perkins and Mrs. Bano Corcellie. Twice a year, Ruby Camino and her husband hosted a dinner for the committee, and the night of October 29th was one of those occasions.

Ruby Camino had cleared the table and was stacking dishes in the kitchen sink when her husband walked in. "How about Monsignor McConnell's tea?" he asked.

"It's on the sideboard in the porcelain teapot the Webster boy gave me," Ruby replied. "I'll bring the coffee in for the others in a minute."

AUTHOR'S NOTE: TWO SEPARATE ACCOUNTS OF WHAT HAPPENED AT THE CAMINO HOUSE IMMEDIATELY FOLLOWING THE LAY COMMITTEE DINNER FOLLOW. THE FIRST ACCOUNT IS FROM GEORGE PERKINS. AT THE TIME, MR. PERKINS WAS AN ENGINEER WITH THE NEW YORK TRANSIT AUTHORITY.

GEORGE PERKINS: "Charley walked back in the room and informed us it would be a few more minutes before Ruby served the coffee. He then went over to the sideboard and picked up a china teapot and a cup. He set them in front of David and left the room to get the cream.

"I was kind of keeping an eye on the Monsignor because he didn't look too good. We all knew he had been on that fast and he looked weak.

"He took the lid off the teapot, removed the tea bag, poured a cup, put in some sugar, stirred it and laid the spoon on the saucer. Then he started to take a sip.

"His hand had just started up with the

cup when all of a sudden it flew up in the air like someone had hit it. The tea splashed out on his face, and he let out a scream. He dropped the cup and toppled backward out of his chair. When he hit the floor, he started rolling around and screaming. His hands were covering his face.

"I jumped up, ran around the table, rolled him over and yelled at Ruby to bring me some ice. I couldn't believe what I saw. It was like someone had poured acid on David's face. His skin was all blistered, and his face had swollen up like a boil. I never saw anything like it."

MRS. BANO CORCELLIE: "The monsignor was talking. I don't think he was paying very much attention to what he was doing, and I don't think he realized that the water in that lovely little teapot was so terribly hot. As he started to take a drink I had the strangest sensation that there was a shudder in the room. I remember seeing the water in my glass tremble. A small amount even splashed out on Ruby's tablecloth. I use to live in California, and we had slight tremors all the time. I guess I didn't think anything of it until I saw the hot tea just leap out of the cup right into his face.

"After George rolled him over, I saw how seriously he was hurt. I remember thinking even then that it was curious that he was only burned in the middle of his face around his features. Another thing that was strange was he didn't spill any on his clothes and there wasn't any on the table. It was almost as if something had directed it right at his eyes, nose and mouth.

"When George Perkins pried his mouth open so he could breathe, I noticed that his tongue was burnt. But I couldn't understand how that could happen because the accident occurred before he ever took a sip."

AUTHOR'S NOTE: ACCORDING TO JOHN KELLY'S NOTES, MRS. CORCELLIE IS THE ONLY ONE WHO REPORTED FEELING THE TREMOR.

Later that evening, Charley Camino returned from the hospital where he and George Perkins had taken Monsignor McConnell. He found his wife waiting for word on the elderly priest's condition.

He reported that McConnell had been treated in the emergency room and admitted for further observation. Because Ruby Camino was in the kitchen at the time of the accident, he attempted to describe the sequence of events that led up to McConnell's accident.

"I just don't understand how such a terrible thing could have happened," Ruby declared.

"I was thinking about that while I was driving home. Do you suppose the handle snapped off the cup?"

"I thought of that, too, but there's no way of knowing. The cup shattered when it hit the floor."

"What about the other cup?" Charley asked.

"Seems strong enough. I tried it after you left for the hospital, and it worked fine."

Charley shook his head. "You know what's weird about this. There were two cups, and the one I gave David is the one I had intended to put at your place at the table. It had a small chip in the saucer, and I knew you'd want David to have the good set. This could just as easily have happened to you."

Both Ruby and Charley gave an almost identical account of what happened later that night.

"We were both asleep when I first heard it. It must have been fairly loud because we're both sound sleepers. I looked over and there was Charley, wide awake, laying there, listening. We could hear a kind of rattling noise coming from the kitchen.

"Charley got out of bed and started downstairs. He keeps a .22 and a flashlight in the stand beside the bed. Our house backs up to the Southern State Parkway, and we've had our house broken into three times since we've lived there. He didn't turn any lights on until he got to the kitchen. I was right behind him. The closer we got, the better we could hear the sound.

"He turned the light on, and there sat the teapot on the counter by the sink. It was rocking back and forth, the way you would expect it to act if some child was playing with it, trying to irritate you. Charley and I looked at each other. Neither of us could believe what we were seeing.

"All of a sudden, the teapot lifted itself right up off the counter, the lid flew off, and the thing shot across the room at us. It missed—but not by much—and smashed against the wall right over my head. If I hadn't ducked, I'm certain it would have hit me.

"Porcelain shattered everywhere. Pieces went all over the kitchen floor, and some of it even went out in the hallway on the carpet. I know it sounds strange, but those fragments of porcelain were so hot that they were smoking. Some of it charred the linoleum in the kitchen, and I've still got little burn marks in the carpet.

"I was afraid that it would catch the house on fire so I bent over and tried to scoop the pieces off the carpet. That's when I burned my hands— third degree burns—and I barely touched them. It was bad enough that I couldn't drive the school bus for almost three weeks."

... DAY EIGHTEEN ...

Some 70-odd people had crowded into the small social hall adjacent to Saint Romaine Roman Catholic Church in Queens following the Requiem Mass celebrated in honor of Vito and Carolyn Messato. Lt. Jerome Steinberg and Fathers Vincent Chiraldi and William Cannon were among them.

Cannon, Steinberg learned, had worked with the Messato couple in several church-authorized psychical investigations and confessed to a great deal of respect for their ability, thoroughness and professionalism. William Cannon had been out of the country prior to the Messato couple's death and returned just in time for the memorial service.

On their way to the church, Vincent Chiraldi

updated his superior on the results of the preliminary investigation into the house. When he
was through, Cannon turned to Steinberg.

"Father Chiraldi tells me you were with Vito
and Carolyn. Is that correct?"

Steinberg nodded. He was surprised that Father Cannon had brought up the subject with so
many people milling about. "Unfortunately, I
was with them every step of the way," he acknowledged.

"Harrowing experience, huh?"

"That's one word for it, but Vincent tells me
the Office of the Chancery won't accept those
kinds of words."

Cannon smiled and reached into his pocket.
He extracted a plain white envelope containing
a three-page typewritten document. "Did Father
Chiraldi tell you about this?"

Steinberg shook his head.

"Good, because I didn't want you to start
asking questions until I had a chance to study it.
It was written by Vito shortly before he took his
life. He was very much the professional, right up
until the end. This document describes everything that went on that afternoon. More impor-
tantly, it details Carolyn's observations as well."

"But Vito told me he didn't get anything on
tape or film."

"That alone tells us something, Lieutenant.
It's quite obvious from this document that both
Vito and Carolyn were convinced we are dealing
with some very powerful influences."

"Over the telephone he speculated that there might be more than one," Steinberg said.

"He believes there are at least two—and perhaps more. The important thing however is the fact that both of the Messatos were convinced that one of the sources represents extreme evil; he called it a very hostile influence."

Steinberg breathed a sigh of relief. Whatever dark forces were playing with Vito Messato's mind prior to his suicide, he still tried to set the record straight before he died.

"When Vito told me the tapes and the film were garbage, I figured we would have to start all over."

"In a sense, Lieutenant, that's exactly what we're going to do. All Vito and Carolyn did was prove that we are not the victims of some hoax. Now the real investigation begins."

Steinberg studied Cannon. He was a stocky man with graying hair and a lantern jaw. He reminded him of a longshoreman with his bull neck and ruddy complexion. He did not, Steinberg had long ago decided, look anymore like a priest than Chiraldi.

"I hear what you're saying," Steinberg acknowledged, "but I'm not sure I understand what you're telling me."

Chiraldi laughed. "What he's telling you, Jerry, is that we'll do what we can to help you."

"What's our first step?"

"Give me a day or two to sift through Vito's report. Let me make my own set of notes and do a little research. Then the three of us will sit down and discuss what we've got. Fair enough?"

"When?"

"How about coming by on Thursday night?" Chiraldi suggested. "I make a mean spaghetti dinner—garlic bread, the works."

Before Steinberg could ask anymore questions, two middle-aged women approached and whisked Cannon away to talk to Vito Messato's mother. Chiraldi and Steinberg were left to themselves.

"Congratulations appear to be in order," Chiraldi said. "It takes a good man to get Bill Cannon to bend the rules; he doesn't do that very often."

"So where do you think he'll start?"

"Same place you and the Messatos did. He'll want to cover the same ground Vito and Carolyn did."

Steinberg wasn't smiling. "Can I tell you something, Vincent? Left to my own devices, I don't think a twenty-mule team could get me back in that house." He tried to work up something that Chiraldi could interpret as a "just kidding" kind of grin, but couldn't pull it off.

"Better brace yourself, my friend," Chiraldi warned him, "because if Cannon decides to get officially involved, that means lots of tours of the house."

The morning of the memorial Mass for Vito and Carolyn Messato, Charla Webster confronted her son with Steinberg's assertions.

Donald, as she anticipated, denied having gone back to the house. When she pressed the issue by insisting that Donald explain where the unfamiliar objects in his room had come from, the boy stormed out of the house, threatening to go live with his father.

Some two hours later, Charla stood in the kitchen and cried. She was looking out the kitchen window, wondering who she could turn to for help, when she saw a figure dart between buildings and enter the side door of the Webster garage. Charla put on her coat and went out to check.

She opened the door and peered into the darkness. The wall switch next to the door did not work. The switch on the far side near the overhead door worked, but she would have to cross the darkened garage to get to it. "Donald?" she asked softly, "are you in here?"

Charla was not prepared for what happened next.

Even though Donald leaped from behind a pile of boxes, he was still partially concealed by shadows. Charla's breath caught in her throat, and her heart began to hammer.

In the half-light she could see the boy's eyes, red and large and terrifying. His mouth hung open, saliva drooling from the corners. He was growling like an animal.

As she took a step toward him, he backed away, moving quickly.

"Donald, what's wrong? Are you all right?"

When she reached out for him again, the boy

jumped back a second time, seeking sanctuary in the uncertainty of the shadows.

Charla's hands were shaking and her knees were trembling.

"Talk to me, Donald. What's wrong?"

The boy lowered his head and snarled. "Leave us alone."

"Us?" Charla repeated. "Is there someone with you?"

"Us," the voice said emphatically. "Now leave us alone."

Charla was terrified and wanted to run. Instead, she began fumbling along the wall for the switch by the overhead door that would transform the world of shadows into light. She stumbled, heard a hiss, regulated her breathing and continued her probe.

"I told you, leave us alone," the voice insisted.

She found the switch, and the cluttered garage was suddenly bathed in light.

Donald was cowering in the corner, shielding his glazed eyes from the sudden brightness. He continued to hiss, emitting a chorus of guttural sounds at his mother, but in the harsh reality of light, he looked merely frightened, like a small boy, pretending and no longer threatening.

"Damn it, Donald, quit that," she shrieked.

The boy continued to cower, inching his way along the back wall of the garage toward a pile of cartons.

Charla told Clara Morrison that she did not know where her strength came from, but she knew she had to conquer her fear. She began walking straight toward her son, trying not to hear the ugly sounds. When she was close enough, she reached out and slapped him across the face.

There was a loud cracking sound. His head snapped back, and his hands flew to his face in defense.

"Stop it," she screamed.

Donald looked up at his mother in stunned silence and crumpled to the oil-stained concrete floor with tears streaming down his face. He curled into the fetal position, and the growls were transformed into whimpers.

Later that afternoon, Charla Webster, after bathing her son and putting him to bed, returned to the only solace she could find. She began to drink. The boy slipped into a deep sleep, and she was alone again.

She used the occasion to search out and round up all of the items she suspected her son had stolen in the past two weeks. She summoned up the strength to return to the garage and was able to come up with only one additional item—an ornate, silver candelabra.

Charla described the candelabra to her aunt over the telephone. It was, she said, very heavy and had a wide, flared base and a twisted stem. "It must have been very expensive," she told her aunt.

After she assembled the items in the kitchen, she fixed herself another drink and sat down to consider her options. One option of course was to call Lt. Steinberg and turn over all of the items to him, but she feared what Steinberg would do with the information. Would he press charges against Donald? Would her son, at only 11 years of age, be put on probation? As alone and confused as Charla was, she knew she could not do that. She would think of something, if she had time.

There was another consideration—the terms of her divorce. What would the courts think and how would they react? She knew that Donald's father would reopen the custody battle if he heard about Donald's behavior. He would charge that his former wife could not control the boy.

The only other option Charla could think of was to have her son return the items he had stolen. That was risky and somewhat frightening in view of Steinberg's repeated warnings. Still, it was more appealing than her other options.

Feeling desperate, Charla called Alice Chambers. For the next several minutes, the two women discussed the feasibility of having their sons return the items stolen from the house at 112 Ocean Avenue.

AUTHOR'S NOTE: A 3 X 5 INDEX CARD WAS STAPLED TO ALICE CHAMBERS' JOURNAL ENTRY FOR OCTOBER 30TH. ON THAT CARD, JOHN KELLY HAD OBVIOUSLY THOUGHT AT SOME LENGTH ABOUT THAT PARTICULAR DIARY ENTRY, AN ACCOUNT OF THE CONVERSATION BETWEEN CHARLA WEBSTER

AND ALICE CHAMBERS EARLIER IN THE AFTERNOON.

HE VIEWED CHARLA WEBSTER AS A VERY LONELY PERSON WHO HARBORED A GREAT MANY INSECURITIES ABOUT ALMOST EVERY ASPECT OF HER LIFE. AT THE TIME THESE EVENTS WERE UNFOLDING, HER PERSONAL AND PROFESSIONAL LIFE WAS IN SHAMBLES. SHE HAD BECOME RECLUSIVE AND RELIED HEAVILY UPON ALCOHOL TO GET HER THROUGH HER DAYS. BOTH OF HER PARENTS WERE DEAD, HER MARRIAGE HAD ENDED IN DIVORCE, AND HER RELATIONSHIP WITH HER SON HAD BEEN STRETCHED TO THE BREAKING POINT. CHARLA WEBSTER COULD POINT TO NO RECENT SUCCESSES.

ON THE OTHER SIDE OF THE SAME CARD, JOHN DREW A PARALLEL BETWEEN CHARLA WEBSTER AND ALICE CHAMBERS. THE CHAMBERS WOMAN WAS CAUGHT UP IN A LOVELESS MARRIAGE AND WAS STRUGGLING TO PLAY THE DIFFICULT ROLE OF SURROGATE MOTHER. ALL OF THIS WAS COMPOUNDED BY HER FEELING A LACK OF FULFILLMENT WITH HER RELIGION.

THE TWO WOMEN, JOHN BELIEVED, COULD HAVE HELPED EACH OTHER IF EVENTS HAD TURNED OUT DIFFERENTLY — BUT THAT TURNING POINT NEVER CAME.

... DAY NINETEEN ...

Charla Webster heard the door shut. Or was it thunder? She sat upright in the bed, cocked her head to one side and listened intently. She realized she wasn't certain what she had heard.

She had been awake for more than an hour listening to the succession of storms hammer at the two-story house. There were frequent and frightening peals of thunder and the alarming sound of the rain as it washed past her window in a seemingly unending string of sporadic downpours.

"Donald?" she called out, "was that you?"

There was no answer.

Sighing, she got out of bed, put on her robe and walked down the hall to her son's room. The room was dark—and Donald was gone. She glanced at the clock on the nightstand beside his bed. The blinking light was an indication that the power had been interrupted at some point during the course of the storm. The numerals indicated that it was 6:31 A.M., but Charla realized it could be later.

Thinking that her son might have gone downstairs to get the morning paper, something he occasionally did on Sunday mornings to read the comics, she went down the stairs and found the house empty. The morning paper was still on the front porch. It was wet, and she left it there.

"Donald," she called again.

No answer.

"Damn him," she muttered. Then she remembered the garage. She went to the kitchen window, looked out at the darkened structure and saw that the side door was standing open. While she watched, Donald emerged, wearing his yellow slicker and carrying a package under his arm. He glanced quickly back at the house, darted out into the alley and disappeared.

In remembering that morning, Charla described herself as still being half-asleep. She rationalized that there were two possibilities, and she wanted to believe the former—that she finally had gotten through to her son and he had gone to early morning Mass. If not, he was blatantly defying her and going back to the house at 112 Ocean Avenue. She could think of no other reason for him to leave the house so early.

Charla went back to her son's room and checked his closet. Perhaps he really had gone to early Mass. When she discovered that his Sunday clothes, a pair of grey trousers and a navy blue blazer, were gone, she was elated. Then, in a typical mother's reaction, she became concerned; with the on-again, off-again nature of the storm she knew he would be drenched by the time he got there.

On a stormy Halloween Sunday morning, Charla went back downstairs. She considered getting dressed and meeting her son at church; then, after Mass, she would buy him breakfast. As she considered her options, she poured her first drink of the day.

Jerome Steinberg also had been awakened by the ferocity of the storm. He had no special plans for the day. It was, as he viewed it, a well-deserved day off, a day he intended to spend cleaning up his condo and perhaps visiting his sister out on the island. He was still considering his options when the phone rang. It was Stephen Carr.

"Thought you were going to get a day off, huh?" Carr said.

"What's up?"

"You know that favorite house of yours, the one on Ocean Avenue?"

"What about it?"

"I just got a call. We've got a unit on the scene for the last hour or so, and it looks like someone is rattling around inside."

"Who's watching it?"

"Ben Lomax of the sheriff's department. He says one minute he sees lights on one floor and the next minute on another."

"What is this, Stephen, some kind of Halloween joke?"

"Afraid not. I'm headed over there. Better meet me."

"I'm on my way," Steinberg said. "I'll be there in thirty minutes."

Steinberg dressed hurriedly without showering or shaving, raced out to his car, and only after turning on the radio learned the extent of the damage caused by the storm. Power had been knocked out over large portions of the eastern half of the island, and there were isolated blackouts in his area as well. Traffic signals were out, street lights flickered, and the streets themselves were deserted. Twice he found it necessary to detour on his way to Ocean Avenue; downed trees and power lines were everywhere.

He arrived at 8:17 A.M. Stephen Carr's unmarked car was parked across the street from the house behind a sheriff's cruiser. Steinberg pulled his car in behind the two cruisers and crawled into the back seat of the deputy's car. Stephen Carr was sitting in the front seat next to Lomax.

Lomax was a burly man of considerable bulk with a bushy beard and a gruff voice. He picked his clipboard up off the dash and verified the time.

"There's a little diner down the street from

here," he said. "I stopped for a cup of coffee, and one of the newscarriers told me he saw some funny lights on in one of the old houses down on Ocean Avenue. When he gave me the address, I checked the O.L. and saw where you guys still had it on the blue list because of the missing priest. So I drove up here. Damned if I didn't see a light in a second floor window in the front. Or at least I thought I did. Another one of them squall lines was moving through just about then and there was a helluva lot of lightning. I couldn't be sure whether I'd seen a light or the reflection of some of the lightning in the window."

"You're positive it wasn't lightning?"

"Damned positive," Lomax grunted. "I pulled over and waited. Sure enough I saw the light again—not lightning."

"Flashlight?"

"Looked more like a candle. Seen it twice since I first reported in. Once on the second floor again and once on the third floor. You could see it move past the window."

"Has to be one or the other," Carr said. "Got a phone call yesterday from your buddy, Chiraldi. He was checking to see if either of us had thought to try the lights when we were in there last time. He wanted permission for him and some guy by the name of Cannon to go through the house. I told him the utilities had been shut off for years."

Steinberg studied the house through the rain. It occurred to him that it could be anyone, either one or both of the two students from Saint Alomar. Neither seemed likely; it was too early in the morning.

"You're certain no one has come or gone since you saw the lights?" Steinberg asked.

Lomax pointed his finger in the direction of the house. "Can't guarantee it, but from where I'm sittin' I can see the front of the house and most of the back. Only way I could have missed 'em is if they came out at the same time one of them squall lines was comin' through."

Carr turned around in the seat. "What do you think?"

"As much as I hate to, I think," Steinberg said, "we better go in and have a look around. Leave Lomax out here to intercept anyone who tries to leave."

Lomax turned on the ignition and pulled his cruiser into the driveway. Carr and Steinberg got out. Just as they did, the skies opened up again. There was a crack of thunder as they made a dash for the back porch. The back door was standing open.

"Son-of-a-bitch," Steinberg muttered, "maybe he's already gone."

Carr flicked on his flashlight and bounced the yellow beam up the hall ahead of them. Steinberg checked out the bathroom and the kitchen. His light created dancing patterns on the mildew-crusted plaster.

"I got a hunch he's still in here," Carr whispered. "The little bastard's overconfident, thinks nobody will be out on a morning like this."

At the foot of the stairs to the second level, the two men stopped. "Did you see that?" Steinberg whispered. "Light, second floor, just for a split second."

"Unless the son-of-a-bitch can see in the dark, he's got to have a light of some kind. If he don't, he stumbles, and then we got his ass."

The two men waited and listened.

"Could have been lightning," Steinberg said.

"Lightning, my ass," Carr grumbled. He moved around Steinberg and started up the stairs. "Cover me. You stay here just in case he gets by me."

Steinberg nodded and edged deeper into the shadows. His back was up against the wall.

When Carr disappeared around the corner at the top of the landing, Steinberg turned off his flashlight and waited. If it was either the Webster or Chambers boy or both he knew they were probably scared. If it was someone—or something—else, a whole new set of problems confronted them.

He could hear Carr moving cautiously across the floor above him.

Even alert as he was, Steinberg was no more prepared for the sudden, violent crash of thunder than he was for the unexpected rapid fire crack-crack-crack of Carr's .38. The two had happened simultaneously.

Steinberg drew his revolver, bolted across the hall and up the steps, bounced off the wall at the landing and took the last six steps three at a time. Carr was just ahead of him, standing halfway up the stairs to the third floor. His revolver hung at his side. He was staring into the grayness at the top of the stairs.

Steinberg looked up and swallowed hard. The candle appeared to be suspended in midair, undulating back and forth.

Carr began backing down the stairs, his eyes still fixed on the candle.

"Christ, Jerry, do you see it?"

Carr had turned his flashlight off, and Steinberg put his hand out to steady the man. "Back down, slowly," he whispered.

"I . . . I put three shots in the damn thing," Carr stammered.

As the two men backed slowly down the stairs, Steinberg became aware of the sickeningly sweet odor. The amorphous vision of an old woman began to materialize. Vagueness became momentary detail, then faded. The specter seemed to come and go, vascillating between a world of reality and nightmare.

The vision consisted of shadows, whispery and spidery threads, tattered and rotting rags.

The candle flickered.

They felt a sudden, icy chill.

The candle went out, and the beam of Steinberg's flashlight was absorbed in the thing that descended the stairs.

Suddenly it began laughing, a derisive and sardonic mocking sound, unfolding its arms to reveal a great mound of flesh hidden in the filthy folds of the rags.

The specter was tearing at that gray, tortured

flesh, clawing at its stomach, as though it was pulling the cancerous growth from it's body. Steinberg could now see that it was the vision of the old woman again. She was giving birth to a creature with a serpentlike head that hissed and made vile sounds. It squirmed and writhed, gyrating obscenely until it began to take another form—the form of a child with a hideous and bulbous head.

Carr backed up, muttering.

The vision held the creature out for them to see and in the process set it free. A serpentlike tongue darted from the tiny creature's mouth, and it excreted a foul-smelling substance as it clawed its way down the front of the woman. Finally it stood defiantly on the steps just above them—hissing, challenging, taunting.

"What the hell is it?" Carr whispered.

"I . . . I wished to hell I knew," Steinberg muttered.

Carr leveled his .38 into firing position again.

"Don't," Steinberg warned him. "It won't help. It's useless."

"What do you mean, it's useless?"

"Because it isn't there," Steinberg started to say—but Carr squeezed off two more shots. The bullets tore into the mucous-like coating that constituted the creature's flesh, and the room was instantly filled with the choking odor of excrement. The thing-child was screeching and threatening.

As it started toward them again, Steinberg

became aware of smoke. It was coming up the stairs at them from the first floor. He looked down and saw that the bottom of the steps was an inferno.

Carr was oblivious to everything except the creature. He raised his revolver a second time and took aim.

"Never mind," Steinberg screamed. "We've got to get out of here." He spun Carr around and pointed at the encroaching flames. "Follow me."

"We can't," Carr shouted. "We can't get through there. We'll have to go out the window."

"Follow me, dammit."

"Christ, Jerry, we'll burn up. We can't make it through that."

"Move, dammit," Steinberg shouted. He grabbed Carr by the arm and jerked him down the stairs and through the wall of flames into the hall leading to the rear door. They clawed their way down the hall onto the back porch, coughing and choking.

Lomax ran to their aid. He dragged Carr down onto the wet grass and saw Steinberg stumble down the porch steps behind him.

"Call the fire department," Carr coughed.

Steinberg reached out and caught Lomax by the sleeve. "Don't. Wait," he said.

Lomax looked at Steinberg and then Carr. He ran up on the porch and shoved the beam of his flashlight down the hall. Then he entered. Minutes later he emerged, his heavily bearded face distorted even further by a perplexed frown. "You must be mistaken, Captain. There's no fire in there. Hell, there ain't even any smoke.

Carr looked at Steinberg. "You had it figured out, didn't you?"

Steinberg nodded. "Yeah, mark it down that for once I was right."

Carr sagged back against the fender of Lomax's patrol car. "Holy shit, Jerry, what kind of thing are we dealing with?"

In nearby Glencoe, Sister Mary Ellen Bertha stood in the vestibule of the mother house looking at the cumbersome, carelessly wrapped package.

"Tell me once again who brought it?"

The novice described, as best she could, the shivering boy who had stood nervously just inside the back door of the novitiate and asked her to give the package to Sister Bertha. "He looked like a drowned puppy. He was so nervous. I asked him his name twice, but he never did tell me."

Sister Bertha shrugged and began unwrapping the unexpected gift. When she saw how lovely the ornate candelabra was, she was pleased.

"Oh, Sister, it is very beautiful," the novice said.

Sister Bertha took the candelabra up to her room and set it in the middle of her small study table. Then she went to find some candles.

. . . DAY TWENTY . . .

Following their 9:00 A.M. Monday morning departmental meeting, Steinberg followed Carr, who was still grousing, into his office. "No progress, no progress, no progress. I might as well buy a damn tape machine and record it or have a rubber stamp made and plaster it all over the update reports."

Steinberg poured himself a cup of coffee. "We don't appear to be making much progress," he admitted. "Answers are slow in coming."

"Slow isn't the word for it," Carr complained. "No trace of Bellini. No trace of Judith Brewer. Not a damn thing to go on. McConnell is no help at all—and then there's that damn house. Each time I go in there I vow I'll never go back."

Carr laughed. "Did you read Lomax's report?"

Steinberg knew what Carr was talking about. "Uh-huh. He didn't even mention the smoke or fire."

"Can't blame him. He didn't see it—we did."

"Or think we did."

"The whole damn thing is weird," Carr said.

"Too many distractions, Stephen. It's like we keep getting off on a tangent, but ultimately everything leads back to that house. And we keep learning the same lesson over and over— that house isn't about to tell us anything."

"You said there were too many distractions. What did you mean?"

Steinberg pursed his lips. "Well, for starters, Sara Wine dug up some interesting information on the Chambers family. Were you aware that Chambers' first wife committed suicide? I dug out the file and went through it last night. The DA came within a whisker of charging Roy Chambers with murder. The only thing that saved Chambers was an undated suicide note."

"Most people don't date suicide notes," Carr said sarcastically. "They've got other things on their mind."

"Sara turned this up. It turns out Monica Chambers wrote suicide notes like some people churn out grocery lists. She did it so often no one took her seriously."

"Go on," Carr said.

"Well, it turns out that one of the boys who

have been stealing things out of that old house is none other than the product of one of Monica Chambers' love affairs. Roy Chambers knew it, and he's been pounding on the kid ever since."

"Like I said, so? What's this got to do with Bellini?"

Steinberg waved his hand. "Maybe nothing—maybe everything. The point is that right in the middle of the Bellini investigation I find what very well could be a ten-year-old unsolved murder."

"Whoa, Jerry, sounds to me like you're jumping to some pretty strong conclusions."

"Am I? Roy Chambers was undergoing psychiatric care when Monica Chambers died. He was also meeting with McConnell on a regular basis. Now, ten years later, he's still taking it out on that kid."

"Have you tried talking to McConnell?"

"McConnell won't talk, and I've got a theory on that, too. I think the Monsignor was counseling Roy Chambers. Chambers gave his wife the overdose of barbiturates and then told McConnell what he did in the confessional."

"Which in effect is as good as sealing McConnell's lips permanently."

"Precisely."

"Still sounds like a long shot," Carr appraised. "What's your next step?"

"I need somebody to pour back through court transcripts, newspaper clippings, talk to Chambers' doctor—leg work."

"I hope you've got an ace up your sleeve."

"I have if you'll call Presley over at the Suffolk County School Corporation and see if he'll loan us Sara Wine for a couple of days. She's already into it, and it would give us a jump start."

"I'll see what I can do. In the meantime, how about Bellini?"

Steinberg sagged. "Yeah, how about Bellini?"

Because of health considerations and her considerable bulk, Sister Bertha was one of the few nuns in the novitiate that used the freight elevator to get from the lobby to her room on the third floor. On the afternoon of Monday, November 1st, she was waiting for that elevator.

Sister Bertha had been looking for an excuse to leave early. Because of that, she had kept a wary eye on the weather throughout the long, depressing day, hoping it would deteriorate so she would have an excuse. If she left her office in Saint Alomar before the last period, she would be able to catch up on some long overdue correspondence. She rationalized that an extra hour was all she needed for a letter to her mother in Montreal and another to her widowed sister in Redwood, California. And, as usual, there were the month-end reports due to the mother house. Since Sister Bertha was beset by constant interruptions in her office at the school, she knew that her room would be the best place to do her paperwork.

The fact that Monsignor McConnell had been incapacitated twice within recent weeks had doubled her work load. She knew there were Saint Alomar reports to file as well.

Sister Bertha dwelled momentarily on the string of disruptions at the Academy in recent weeks. First there was Father Bellini's sudden disappearance. Then the Monsignor had been scalded by tea. Now Ruby Camino had been burned bad enough that she couldn't drive her school bus, and Sister Bertha had a difficult time locating a substitute driver.

As she stepped from the elevator, she encountered two young teaching novices, recently arrived from the order's central mother house in Portland. The girls, Canadian like herself, were laughing and cavorting in the hallway. She scowled her disapproval of their frivolous behavior and retired to her room.

Both novices later recalled that they were surprised to see the Mother Superior so early in the afternoon. It was shortly before 3:00 P.M., and the last class at Saint Alomar wasn't dismissed until 3:20.

It was customary for all members of the order to convene for prayer one hour prior to dinner. Each month, a different member of the house was assigned the responsibility of making the announcements and discussing the order's concerns before the commencement of the prayer hour. The announcements covered individual assignments as well as parish and school obligations. Sister Bertha was charged with this responsibility for the month of November. When it came time for the announcements and the other members of the order were assembled, Sister Bertha had not arrived. A novice was sent to remind Sister Bertha of the hour.

The novice went to the third floor room and knocked twice. There was no answer. She called out the sister's name, but still there was no answer.

She tried the door, but it was locked. Novice Wallace was surprised. It was against the order's rules to lock any interior door in the novitiate. Confronted with no answer and a locked door, the young woman went for help.

She returned several minutes later with Sister Frances Allaina and Sister Carla Birdsong. The latter, using a master key, gained access to Sister Bertha's room. They all were concerned because Sister Bertha had a history of heart trouble. Sister Birdsong later admitted that she feared the worst even before entering the room.

They found Sister Bertha sitting at her desk in front of the window overlooking the austere Saint Alomar courtyard. In the middle of the study table, Sister Bertha was burning a candle in her new candelabra. Along with a small desk lamp it provided the only illumination in the room.

Sister Mary Bertha was dead, her vacuous eyes fixed on the emptiness beyond her window. Sister Birdsong checked for a pulse. Finding none, she fell to her knees in prayer.

Later, after Sister Bertha's body had been removed, Sister Birdsong attempted to tidy up the dead woman's room. She read the salutation on the letter that Sister Bertha had just begun. It was addressed to her mother.

"Mother," the letter began, "I know you will be happy to hear that I will be coming home soon." The word "home" was distorted, and the word "soon" deteriorated into an ugly scrawl.

Sister Birdsong, who was Sister Bertha's closest confidant and dearest friend at the time of her death, would later state that she was not aware of Sister Bertha's plans to visit Montreal anytime in the near future.

AUTHOR'S NOTE: PERHAPS THE READER WILL BE INTRIGUED BY THE FACT THAT SISTER BERTHA'S SALUTATION TO HER MOTHER PROVED TO BE CHILLINGLY PROPHETIC. SHE WAS BURIED IN THE FAMILY PLOT OF THE MAISON CEMETERY NEAR MONTREAL, NEXT TO THE PLACE DESIGNATED FOR HER MOTHER. ("HOME".)

THE DEATH CERTIFICATE OF SISTER MARY ELLEN BERTHA INDICATES THAT DEATH WAS DUE TO A CORONARY OCCLUSION AT APPROXIMATELY 4:00 P.M. ON MONDAY, NOVEMBER 1ST.

ON THE REVERSE SIDE OF THE PHYSICIAN'S REPORT, ATTACHED TO THAT DEATH CERTIFICATE, THERE IS A NOTE. "THE DECEASED'S EYES SHOW EVIDENCE OF SEVERE RETINA DAMAGE—PROBABLY THE RESULT OF PROLONGED EXPOSURE TO AN INTENSE OPEN FLAME."

. . . DAY TWENTY-ONE . . .

At Mass prior to the first class of the day at Saint Alomar, the students watched Monsignor David McConnell walk somberly down from the altar to the communion railing before the benediction. The Monsignor, face bandaged, cleared his throat. "I have an announcement to make," he said. "We are deeply saddened by the untimely death of Sister Mary Ellen Bertha. Sister Bertha was beloved by the faculty, staff and the entire student body. Please bow your heads and join me in prayer for the repose of her soul."

McConnell closed his eyes and bowed his head. Then, when the silent prayer was over, he returned to the altar for the benediction.

Only then did Lester steal a glance at Kooch Webster sitting beside him. Kooch's face was

encased in a thoroughly delighted smile.
Kooch's small fist slapped down on his knee.
"Way ta go," he said, grinning.

Alice Chambers stayed for Mass after driving
the two boys to school. After hearing the announcement of Sister Bertha's sudden passing,
she left the sanctuary and stopped at the Saint
Alomar novitiate. Alice May had frequently
worked with the Mother Superior during her
own tenure at Saint Alomar, and she wanted to
convey her condolences to the other nuns in the
order. Sister Birdsong was teaching at the academy, so only Sister Frances Allaina was there to
greet her. The two women embraced briefly and
then discussed how their former colleague had
died.

Sister Allaina showed Alice May the room
where Sister Bertha had died, and the two
women knelt down on the floor of the room and
prayed.

One of the November 2nd entries in Alice
Chambers' journal describes her visit to the
novitiate and contains the following observations:

*"I found the stark surroundings of Mary
Bertha's room to be a disquieting reminder of
my own troubled final days in the order. I
could not help but notice the orderly manner
in which she kept her reading and how neatly
her personal effects were arranged and accounted for. The glass crucifix that I gave her*

several years ago was still hanging over her desk. Only the ornate candelabra seemed out of place in these humble surroundings and the manner in which she lived.

"I realize that objects, in and of themselves, are neither intrinsically good or inherently evil. Yet, as I looked at that candelabra, I sensed something. Perhaps the word I should use is unpleasant, because I hesitate to use a word so strong as evil. Yet evil is clearly the sense it gave me.

The three men retired to Cannon's study. Chiraldi provided the Drambuie and Cannon the cigars. Steinberg recalls that evening as an oasis in a string of misfortunes.

"So," Steinberg said, getting down to business, "should I assume you've had the opportunity to digest Vito Messato's report by now?"

"I have," Cannon admitted while he stoked the fire. "In fact, I've gone a step further. I've notified my superiors that Father Chiraldi and I intend to conduct an investigation."

"Do they have to bless it?"

Chiraldi laughed. "I like the play on words."

"Actually, letting them know is just a courtesy," Cannon admitted. "They know they're too far away from the action to make an assessment. We should be able to get started within the week. Their permission to start is a mere formality."

"Sounds like you're dealing with as big a bureaucracy as I do," Steinberg said.

"Bigger," Chiraldi said.

"Vincent tells me you had the occasion to go back in the house."

Steinberg nodded and explained what had happened. He concluded with the omission in Lomax's report. "I think he thinks Carr and I were hallucinating."

"Were you?" Cannon asked.

"I don't know what we were doing. I do know I saw flames and smelled smoke. I even felt the heat. But when someone checks the place out a few minutes later and finds nothing, you begin to question yourself."

"Was there anything different this time compared to the last—heat versus cold, noise versus silence—that sort of thing?"

Steinberg thought for a moment. "Maybe the vision, or whatever it was, was a little more intense. Maybe I could see it clearer."

"Could it be that you understood what you were seeing a little better?" Cannon asked.

"Perhaps. It was pretty vivid. Vincent keeps cautioning me about using the wrong words, but the best way to describe it is scary."

"Well, maybe the influence has figured out it's going to take a little more to scare you and your friend Carr off?" Chiraldi laughed.

"That's exactly the feeling I get, Vince. Whatever or whoever it is doesn't want us in there."

"Father Chiraldi is right, Lieutenant. They do try harder and harder. The next time it will probably be worse."

Steinberg took a sip of the amber liqueur and

lit his cigar. "If there is a next time," he muttered.

"What about the role of Monsignor McConnell in all of this?" Cannon asked. His question caught Steinberg by surprise.

Steinberg looked at Chiraldi. The young priest had obviously relayed his complaints about McConnell's reluctance to do anything to help the investigation. "He hasn't been much help," he admitted.

"Monsignor McConnell is one of the people I intend to talk to," Cannon said. "I feel certain that when he understands what's happening, he'll be eager to cooperate."

Chiraldi squatted on his haunches in front of the fireplace and poked at the fire. "Now is as good time as any, Jerry. Why don't you ask him?"

Cannon looked up from his drink. "Ask me what?"

Steinberg hesitated, but Cannon's level gaze encouraged him. "It's a long way around the barn."

"Give me a good story and good cigar and I'm all ears, Lieutenant."

Slowly and carefully, Steinberg took Cannon through the convoluted trail of his suspicions about Roy Chambers and the death of his first wife. He concluded with what Sara Wine had uncovered in her investigation and his conversation with Stephen Carr.

"Interesting story, Lieutenant, and you say

David McConnell was this man Chambers' spiritual counselor through all of this?"

"Originally there was a psychiatrist involved, but Roy Chambers quit going to him shortly before his wife died. At the time Monica Chambers is supposed to have taken her life, the only help Chambers was getting was coming from Monsignor McConnell."

"How certain are you of what you just told me?"

"It all happened ten years ago, Father. The trail is old, and the memories are short. There are ways of going back and digging it all out, but I don't know how much time we have."

Cannon arched his eyebrows. "I'm not sure I know what you're getting at, Lieutenant."

"I think there is someone who really knows what happened to Monica Chambers. I think he knows because I think Roy Chambers revealed what really happened in the confessional."

"If that's the case, Lieutenant, then we will never know, will we?"

"Under what circumstances would McConnell be obliged to reveal what he knows?"

"There are no circumstances, Lieutenant. David McConnell has taken a very sacred vow, a vow that outweighs the moral and legal dilemmas we so often find ourselves in."

"This isn't new, Jerry. We live with this one day in and day out," Chiraldi said.

"I figured as much. Which may explain why McConnell refuses to talk about Father Bellini."

"Connect the two," Cannon said.

"I was testing what I had heard about the sanctity of the confessional. If McConnell won't talk about Chambers, he won't talk about Father Bellini."

"I'm afraid I still don't see the connection."

"When you do an investigation, Father, two things happen. You uncover some of the things you're looking for, and you get a few surprises. There is a persistent rumor that Father Bellini was seeing a young woman by the name of Judith Brewer."

"You suspect an affair?" Cannon asked.

Steinberg shrugged. "Who knows? But when you're a cop your mind works like this. Suppose Bellini was having an affair, and suppose he told McConnell all about it in the confessional. McConnell couldn't talk about it, could he? So how does he handle it? He makes himself unavailable by fasting. And then he has the perfect out. Because Bellini's car is found in the driveway of the same house that caused all that fuss more than a decade ago, he can dismiss the whole thing as—and I'm using his words— 'superstitious rubbish.' "

"And you think that's why David isn't cooperating?"

Steinberg laughed. "By now you can tell, Father, I don't know what I think. Does Bellini's disappearance have anything to do with Leon Silverman? What happened to Carolyn Messato? Does any of it tie to anything?"

THE NIGHTMARE CONTINUES

"Well, Lieutenant, I can tell you one thing with some degree of certainty."

"What's that?"

"Father Chiraldi and I will get a handle on that house for you—but I'm afraid the rest of it is up to you."

. . . DAY TWENTY-TWO . . .

Wednesday, November 3rd, began as many days had during the previous two weeks in Amityville—overcast and unpleasant. A chill wind blew in off the bay from the south, and the temperature hovered just above freezing. The day was punctuated alternately by periods of sleet, snow flurries and cold, dismal rain. It was, Charla Webster decided, a day consistent with her prospects—gloomy. She was contemplating a call to Lt. Steinberg.

Her son's mysterious Sunday morning excursion was still very much on her mind. When he returned home that day and was confronted by her, he denied any wrongdoing. He used the opportunity to slip even further into a secretive and noncommunicative posture. Their confrontation ended as it had on two other recent occasions, with Charla striking her son and sending him to his room.

The boy refused to talk to her for the balance of that day and for the two following days. Only after hearing of the death of Sister Bertha did Donald brighten. Charla did not understand why, but she suspected that her son had returned to the house on Ocean Avenue.

The previous evening, while Donald was cloistered in his room, she went to the garage and discovered where two additional items had been cached—an antique clock with a chipped and sooty glass face, and a small imitation leather jewelry box. The latter contained an assortment of tarnished men's accessories.

In a frame of mind that she would describe as being "at wit's end" and with no one else to talk to, Charla decided to call Steinberg and inform him she was certain her son had stolen additional items from the house. She hoped that a confrontation between her son and the officer would persuade Donald to change his behavior.

"Lt. Steinberg, please," she said when the station clerk answered.

The officer came on the line moments later. "Steinberg."

"Lieutenant, this is Charla Webster." Then she added, as if her name might need further explanation, "Donald's mother."

"What can I do for you, Mrs. Webster?"

It had taken Charla a long time to work up the courage to call the officer, and now that she had finally taken the step, she did not hesitate. "I think my son has gone back to that old house, Lieutenant. I've found several things in the garage that don't belong to us."

Steinberg listened. If nothing more than this came from the call, he now knew which of the boys was continuing to steal from the house.

"Will you talk to him?" she pleaded. "Maybe it will put the fear of the law in him."

"If you think it will help. When would you like me to do it?"

When Steinberg agreed, Charla felt as if a burden had been lifted from her shoulders, and she regained a degree of composure. "At your convenience, Lieutenant. I would be most grateful."

"How about this evening? I drive right past your place on my way home."

Charla felt relieved. Steinberg represented help. A time of 6:30 P.M. was confirmed, and she thanked him and hung up. Then she called the only other person Charla is known to have confided in during this period—her aunt, Clara Morrison.

At the Saint Alomar rectory, Father William Cannon waited in the library while Mrs. Heart informed Monsignor McConnell that the representative of the Chancery had arrived.

Cannon had been informed of McConnell's most recent misfortune when he called to arrange the meeting. "Tell David this won't take long," he said abruptly. Cannon did not allow

Mrs. Heart the time to expound on the Monsignor's condition.

On three things everyone who knew Father Cannon agreed; he was curt, pointedly honest and short on the social graces.

McConnell had been unable to shave since the accident in the Camino house, and he was aware that he was unable to present himself in a favorable light. He was wearing trousers, a tee shirt, a dark robe and slippers, and his demeanor was less than affable. There was still a large inflamed area around his mouth, and numerous pinpoint facial blisters gave testimony to the severity of his burns. He was still experiencing some difficulty in communicating. When Cannon heard him speak, he realized that the Monsignor had received burns inside his mouth as well.

Visits by representatives of the Chancery were usually less than cordial affairs, and McConnell was naturally apprehensive. He was concerned that Cannon might be probing into the disappearance of Father Bellini. Even McConnell, who was usually shielded from such gossip, had started to hear talk about the young priest's indiscretions. If that was what Cannon wanted to talk about, he would simply tell him that he was unable to discuss his former assistant's behavior. He was certain Cannon would understand.

On the other hand, if Cannon was looking into the death of Sister Bertha, he was prepared to assure him that there were no extenuating circumstances surrounding the Mother Superior's passing.

McConnell took a seat. "Mrs. Heart informs me you were quite insistent, Father. Is there a problem?"

As usual, Cannon went straight to the heart of the matter. To McConnell's chagrin, he didn't even take time to inquire into the Monsignor's health. "Are you aware, Monsignor, that within the last two weeks, the office of the Chancery has had two separate requests to look into the current situation at the old house on Ocean Avenue?"

"Not again," McConnell sighed. "When will people let it rest?"

"I'm certain that you have heard some of the—"

"Rubbish," McConnell snarled. "I've heard rubbish and jibberish. Is that what this visit is about?"

"I take it the reports are true then, Monsignor. Two different sources have informed us that you have been unwilling to make even a preliminary assessment of the situation." To McConnell's surprise, Cannon's initial thrust was even more brusque than usual.

"I would like to think the office of the Chancery has more important matters to tend to than chasing down inane rumors."

"Inane?" Cannon repeated. "Rumors?"

"Certainly. Inane is the appropriate word for it. The reports are pure poppycock. Consider who you have heard this from—Alice Chambers, no doubt. And if you're telling me that the Chancery is investigating this matter based on what you've heard from Alice Chambers, I can assure you, you are wasting both our time. The fact of the matter is I can defuse your concerns in thrity seconds and bring this matter to a very swift conclusion."

"Please do then, Monsignor. But before you do, let me tell you that Mrs. Chambers is not the only party we've heard from. There has been an official police request as well."

McConnell stammered. "The only reason the police are involved is because Father Bellini's car was found in the driveway of the same house the day he disappeared."

"On the contrary, Monsignor, the police are involved for an entirely different reason. During the course of their investigation into Father Bellini's disappearance they learned that items were being stolen from the same property where Bellini's car was found. As it turns out, one of those stolen items was used to kill a pawnshop owner in Amityville."

McConnell blinked than stiffened. "I fail to see—" He was cut off by Cannon before he could finish.

"The police are certain two Saint Alomar students are involved with those thefts."

"More rubbish. It's merely an attempt to smear the name of our fine school."

"On the contrary, Monsignor, I see a need for

cooperation between the Church and local officials. It's a shame you don't see it the same
way."

McConnell bristled. "Are the police prepared
to give us the names of the offending students?"

"Damn it, David, you're missing the point.
The police do not want to take action against
those students. They want the thefts stopped,
and they want our cooperation. And the cooperation they've requested is nothing more than
our assistance in helping them investigate that
house. That is a very old house, David, and
someone could get hurt. Do I have to point out
that it could be your students who are the ones
that get hurt?"

McConnell glared at the Chancery representative. He tried to modulate his voice. "You and I
are intelligent men, William, and I might go so
far as to add, rational and God-fearing men. As
such, we both know there is nothing to the
persistent talk about that house. Don't you see
that it's a scheme, a scheme to make money or
gain publicity?"

"How can you be so sure, David?"

McConnell looked away.

Cannon later explained that he took his job
seriously. He viewed his responsibility as being
the audit functionary for a management that
was headquartered thousands of miles away in
Rome. It was his job to make certain that the
priests were doing their job correctly. In that
capacity, he could not allow himself to be im-

pressed with titles. The fact that McConnell held the rank of Monsignor was not allowed to deter him.

"Let me caution you, Father Cannon, if you are considering a Church-sanctioned investigation of the former Defio house based on the babblings of Alice Chambers, I can assure you that you will become the laughingstock of the community. In the process, you will publicly humiliate this institution as well."

"I've read the files on the former Sister Mary Alice, the one you call Mrs. Chambers."

"Then you know that she was a member of the order that is responsible for the high academic standards of Saint Alomar. And, if you've really looked into the matter, you are also aware that Alice Chambers is a very unstable individual."

"That is a serious charge, David."

"Let me give you the real facts, Father, not the couched semantics of a personnel file. At the time Alice Chambers relinquished her place in the order, she was under my personal scrutiny. Plainly speaking, her work with the students was unacceptable. She repeatedly demonstrated signs of psychological instability. At the time she chose to leave the order I had already spoken to the Mother Superior about having her reassigned. And that reassignment, Father, would only have been appropriate if it had been to the order's Mother House where she could rest."

"Did you inform her of this when she resigned?"

"I saw no need to share the depth of my investigation, but I cautioned her that life outside the order would be even more stressful than what she was undergoing."

Cannon was taking notes. He laid his pen down. "Are you telling me that you declined to forward her request for assistance to the Chancery on the ground that you personally considered her to be psychologically unstable?"

"In so many words, yes."

"Are you working from some psychological assessment that I don't have access to?"

"I do not need psychological assessments, Father. I know what I was seeing. She was a poor performer. She rattled easily. She was extremely nervous. She was unstable. These things were easy to see. Following up on her request would have been a waste of time. I was here during the last circus surrounding that old house. I'm ashamed to admit that I even know Father Mancuso. He should not have allowed himself to become involved in such a blatant travesty. It was a hoax. It ruined him."

"Hoax?" Cannon repeated.

"It was clearly a hoax. An obvious attempt by charlatans to imply demonic involvement—a most unfortunate occurrence, the stuff of overactive imaginations."

"Is that how you would describe Lt. Steinberg?"

"Steinberg is an impertinent young man who allows his authority to go to his head. He disobeyed me. He sought permission to take this matter to the Chancery, and I denied it. Then he had the gall to go over my head and seek out your office without my permission."

Cannon's voice was even. "I believe that Lt. Steinberg was only doing his job, Monsignor. The way I see it, he tried to work within the constraints of the relationship between church and state as defined by the Church itself."

"And you, Father Cannon are obviously a poor judge of character."

Cannon was implacable. "I must ask you these questions, David. I have a report to file. First, why were you unwilling to relay two requests for assistance to the office of the Chancery? Secondly, why this hostility toward Alice Chambers? Is your disappointment at being unable to convince her to remain in her order so great that you have turned your back on her?"

McConnell's shoulders sagged. "There are aspects of both the Chambers and Bellini situations that I am unable to discuss."

"Let me make sure I understand you, David— unable or won't?"

"I have taken vows, as you have."

"I won't let you hide behind that, David. The fact remains that Lt. Steinberg came to you after two separate visits to that house. This was not a casual request. Steinberg and a fellow officer both witnessed what I feel even you would have to regard as evidence that would lend their request credibility."

"Do you actually believe a mere policeman would know the difference between an influence and a hoax?"

"On one of his investigations he was accompanied by the Messatos."

"I have never shared your office's enthusiasm for the work of the Messatos."

Cannon laid his pad aside and opened his briefcase. "Here, David, read this sometime. It was written by Vito Messato just before he died. After you've read it, I believe you will see what an error in judgment you've made. If you had cooperated with Lt. Steinberg, this whole affair would probably have been behind us."

McConnell leaned forward, his voice a barely audible hiss. "Now, let me tell you something, Father Cannon. I have every intention of filing my own report with the diocesan office. Mine will not be based on conjecture; mine will be based on fact."

"Never mind the posturing, David. I'm not impressed. My concern is determining what is going on in that house. And if you are smart, you will be just as concerned as I am."

Later that day, while relaying his conversation with McConnell to Father Chiraldi, Cannon would laugh and say he hoped he had stirred up McConnell enough to get him "off his butt."

Still later that day, Cannon informed the diocesan office that the office of the Chancery would conduct a thorough investigation of the house on Ocean Avenue. "I have," Cannon told

Chiraldi, "too much respect for Carolyn and Vito Messato not to. That is the least we owe them."

"Pssst." Kooch was trying to get Lester's attention from across the table. Lester was trying equally hard to ignore him.

"So what do you think now?" Kooch whispered.

Lester rolled his eyes. "Awww, forget it. Let it go."

"Didn't I tell you the stuff was haunted?"

Lester was thinking about moving to another study table.

"Bertha's dead, ain't she?"

Lester looked around the room. Kooch was making him nervous. They were in the school library and students were not permitted to talk while they were seated at the study tables. Lester pointed to the "SILENCE" sign. "Keep it up and you'll get us thrown out of here."

To Lester's chagrin, Kooch got up, walked around the table and sat down next to him. He propped a large geography book up in front of his face so that Sister Karen would not be able to see who was talking.

"I'm tellin' ya, ya shoulda seen it. I put on quite a show. I got up real early Sunday, got dressed like I was going to Mass, and then I timed it so I showed up at the back door of the novitiate at the same time Mass let out. When I knocked on the door, some novice answered. I gave her the package and told her it was for Sister Bertha. That candlestick is what did it, man. It zapped her off, just like I said it would."

Lester couldn't resist. "Awww, Kooch, yer lying. I heard a couple of the nuns talking after catechism class; they said Sister Bertha died of a heart attack."

Kooch jabbed Lester with his elbow. "You're a dumb ass, Lester, know that? Don't ya see? That is what they want ya to believe. Nuns never admit it when anything goes wrong."

"How come?" Lester asked.

"That's the way they teach 'em."

There was a louder than usual shushing sound from the front of the room. Lester could tell that Sister Karen had the voices isolated.

"You don't believe it, do ya?" Kooch hissed. "Know why? Because you're just as dumb as the rest of them."

Lester was still trying to think of a comeback when he realized that Sister Karen had out-flanked them. She was right behind Kooch and was sporting her 18-inch wooden ruler with the steel edge. Lester had been around Saint Alomar long enough to know the librarian never missed once she had zeroed in on her target.

The ruler crashed down on the back of Lester's blackened hand, and an angry red welt appeared instantly. The attempt to mete out the same punishment to Kooch wasn't as success-ful. Kooch dodged to one side and caught her hand on the downswing. He plucked the ruler out of the nun's hand and hurled it across the room. It ricocheted off of the blackboard and clattered to the floor.

Lester looked sheepishly around the room. Everyone was looking at them. Most of them were afraid to smile, but he knew what they were thinking. They were glad it was him instead of them.

Kooch's triumph was short-lived. Sister Karen was too agile. One hand pinned Kooch to the study table, and the other jerked his chair out from under him. He went to his knees, chin on the table, howling. This time when Lester looked around, the other kids were smiling.

Five minutes later they were in McConnell's office, and the Monsignor was glaring at them. "Now, Mr. Webster, you and I are going to have a little talk." He shoved Donald into a straightback chair and pinned the palm of his hand against the boy's chest. To Lester's complete amazement, the Monsignor seemed to have forgotten all about him.

McConnell was already breathing hard.

"So, you want to talk, Mr. Webster? Well, why don't you talk to me?"

Kooch glared back at his tormentor. "Get your hands off of me, fatso."

McConnell's hand crashed down against the side of the boy's face, and Kooch's head snapped back. The Monsignor's face was flushed. "Talk, Mr. Webster, talk. Tell me what was so important."

"Leave me alone, old man." Kooch demanded.

"Talk to me, Mr. Webster," McConnell screeched, "and while you're at it, tell me about all the things you and Lester have been stealing." The Monsignor was having trouble breathing.

Kooch's lips were sealed.

Lester was on the verge of stepping forward and telling McConnell what he wanted to know, but McConnell's hand came crashing down again, almost knocking Kooch off of the chair.

"Stop," Lester shouted. "He—he was just tellin' me how Sister Bertha died."

"What about Sister Bertha?" McConnell demanded.

Lester was trembling. "He said—said she—she didn't die of a heart attack."

McConnell straightened up. The network of blisters and scabs on his face made him look all the more terrifying. "That's very interesting, Mr. Webster. Since you seem to know so much about it, why don't you tell us how Sister Bertha died?"

From the look on his face, Lester decided Kooch was finally losing some of his bravado. He was certain he saw tears in Kooch's eyes.

"Talk," McConnell screamed.

When McConnell raised his hand again, Lester blurted it out. "He's got some crazy idea about the stuff he's been stealin' being haunted."

Kooch scowled up at his friend. "I'll get you for this, fart face."

Even the burns on McConnell's face couldn't

266

hide his expression of satisfaction. He had exactly what he needed. Now he could expel Donald Webster. He stepped back and allowed his seething anger to dissipate into a broad, obscene smile. "Well, well, well, Mr. Webster—so it is true. You *have* been stealing from that old house."

Lester swallowed hard. Things were turning out all wrong again.

McConnell walked to the door, turned and pointed at Kooch. "I'm leaving to call your mother, Mr. Webster. When I reach her I will inform her that you are no longer a student at Saint Alomar. You have been expelled for theft and insubordination."

Lester didn't know what insubordination meant, but he figured it had something to do with Kooch calling McConnell "fatso." The theft part he understood.

The Monsignor turned toward Lester. "And don't think I've forgotten about you, young man. I'll deal with you later."

As Lester started to leave Kooch looked up at him. "Nice going, fat ass. Now you got me in real trouble."

Jerome Steinberg crawled out of his car in front of the Webster home a few minutes early. It had been a long day, and he was tired. The stop at the Webster household was the last remaining barrier between Steinberg and a hot shower. He hoped Charla Webster was not expecting an eloquent dissertation on the evils of theft. He planned to do nothing more than to explain to the boy that he had to stay away from the house. Ten minutes was all Steinberg figured it would take, and he would be on his way again.

He stepped up on the porch and rang the doorbell. Charla barely opened the door, studying him through the narrow opening.

"It's me, Mrs. Webster, Jerry Steinberg. You asked me to stop by this evening to talk to your son. Remember?"

Charla stared back at him, her eyes glazed. She had been crying and had been drinking. "That—that won't be necessary—now," she slurred.

Steinberg started to ask why, but she cut him off.

"It's too late for talk, Lieutenant, much too late." She closed the door.

Later Steinberg would recall that he stood there for several minutes feeling foolish. He lit a cigarette and waited, but she did not return. Finally he turned and started for his car. As he did, he shouted back over his shoulder. "And tell him he better return the things he took out of that house."

As he turned the key in the ignition, he wondered if Charla Webster had heard him.

... DAY TWENTY-THREE ...

Charla Webster did not go to work on Thursday, November 4th. Instead, she phoned her office shortly after 8:00 A.M. and informed her supervisor that she had to take Donald to the doctor. "I will be in," she told him, "as soon as I get him home and find someone to stay with him." Charla's supervisor, like the rest of the people in her office, was aware of the difficulties she had with her son since her mother died.

Donald, of course, was not sick. Charla simply had no place to turn. His expulsion from Saint Alomar only compounded her problems. If she went to work, the boy would be unsupervised for over ten hours, and Charla did not feel she could take that risk.

The woman's problems with her son, Steinberg later learned, were further compounded by a relationship at her place of employment. The situation was cumbersome for both her and her department head, Charles Griffin. The two had a brief affair shortly after Charla began working there, several months before her divorce was finalized. It ended in acrimony.

Charla's situation was made even more difficult by the fact that the firm was undergoing an austerity program, and department heads had been told to weed out employees who were performing at less than a high level of efficiency.

Griffin had informed Charla of this impending action and advised her that her current level of performance was less than satisfactory, citing her handling of the Boston case and frequent absences because of excessive drinking and personal problems with her family. Believing that their former relationship and not her performance was at the heart of the matter, Charla disregarded the warnings and threatened to go to the firm's founder with the real story. She is said to have told Griffin, "If I go down, you go down with me."

That morning, Griffin told her, "I can cover for you for awhile, but you better get in here as quick as you can. We're having a meeting on the Boston case this afternoon, and your report still isn't ready."

Charla hung up from the unsettling call,

walked slowly into the kitchen and poured herself a cup of coffee. Her son was upstairs asleep. She, on the other hand, had been up most of the night, worrying. Even with her night-long vigil, she was no closer to finding a solution to her dilemma. She realized that Donald would have to be enrolled in a new school as quickly as possible, but the options presented her with other problems. She did not feel that a public school would be the answer because she did not believe Donald would receive the necessary guidance and supervision. Another Catholic Academy was out of the question because of the cost. Saint Alomar was the least expensive private school in the area. Between child support payments and her salary, she could barely afford the Saint Alomar tuition. A school further out on the island, with all of the attendant logistical problems of getting Donald back and forth, was also out of the question.

There were, of course, other possibilities, but she had not explored them yet. She hoped to use the day to work her way through some of these problems. Donald could be sent back to live with his father—if his father would take him. He had contested the settlement that awarded custody of Donald to his former wife at the time the divorce was finalized. But that was almost a year ago, and neither Charla nor her son had heard from the man in quite some time. There were rumors that Donald's father had moved to New Jersey. If so, it would make it all the more difficult for her to turn the boy over to him; state boundaries were involved.

Selling her recently purchased house was another option. She could sell the house and move in with Clara Morrison, who was alone and saddled with the responsibility of a large home. There was more than enough room for Charla and the boy, but Charla was concerned about her privacy.

Perhaps the most appealing option at the moment was leaving the Long Island area altogether—a new job for her and a new school for Donald. It was appealing because she felt it had the advantage of solving all of her problems at once.

Unfortunately, Charla was not of the frame of mind to address her problems. That morning, all of her options appeared to be fatally flawed by time, by money or by her son.

She was not surprised when she looked up and saw him standing in the doorway, glowering defiantly at her. "I don't care what that cop said. I'm not taking that stuff back to that old house."

Donald was referring to their conversation the previous evening when Charla learned of her son's expulsion and informed him that he would have to return everything he had stolen before she would look into the matter of getting him back in school. "I've already made arrangements to help you take them back. Your Aunt Clara is going to help us."

"Why take that junk back?" he complained.

"Nobody lives there, so nobody cares what happens to all that stuff."

As weary as Charla felt, she was still determined. "You will return them, and you will return them *today*. You'll put everything back, right where you found it."

The boy continued to glare at her. "I won't do it," he said.

Donald's continued defiance brought about the only retaliation Charla felt she had left to her disposal. She slapped him across the face, the force of the blow knocking the boy down. In a fit of profanity, he scrambled to his feet and bolted from the room. Charla heard him race up the steps and the door to his room slam behind him.

Charla was still contemplating her next move when the phone rang. The stress in her voice was all too evident when she answered. It prompted Clara Morrison to ask, "Are you alright, dear?"

Based on her niece's response, Clara determined that she should hurry over to the Webster household. She was afraid that if she didn't, a despondent Charla would start drinking, and the day would be a total loss for the distraught woman.

By noon, the two women had placed all of the stolen items in a cardboard box and stored them in the trunk of Clara Morrison's car. Then they went back into the house to escape the chill November air.

While Clara waited, Charla went upstairs to get her son. The door was locked.

"Donald, everything is loaded in the car; we're ready to go."

She was not surprised when the boy did not answer.

"Donald, do you hear me?"

Again there was no answer.

"It won't do any good to balk. Everything is loaded. Let's get it over with."

Charla could hear her son moving about in the room and tried the door a second time.

Her patience was already worn thin as the result of their earlier encounter. "Donald, damn it, open this door." To her astonishment the door began to creak open. It wasn't until she had entered the room that she felt the chill. She could hear the sound of wind, and the cold was stinging her face. She glanced at the windows, which were closed. Despite that, there was the howling sound of a storm, growing more fierce by the moment. She looked at Donald, who was sitting in the middle of the floor and appeared to be in a trance. There were large, discolored circles around the boy's eyes, and the pupils were crimson. His jaw was hanging open as though it had been unhinged.

She took a step toward him. "Donald, what is the matter?"

The sound he made was catlike, the gesture being that of a cat as well. He clawed at her as though to ward her off.

Charla managed to stifle a scream, but Donald's hissing sounds filled the room.

"Go away. Leave us alone." The words came out of his mouth, but it was not his voice. The voice Charla heard was pregnant with loathing.

She sensed her son's malevolence and picked up the first thing she could find to defend herself. It was Donald's hockey stick. As he began to crawl toward her, she arched the club over her head. He coiled and crouched, preparing, she thought, to attack. She arched the stick down with all the strength she could muster. It was a glancing blow, off the boy's shoulder. She brought the club back and arched it down again. The second blow caught him across the back. He spun, continued the hissing sound and clawed out at her.

"Donald!" she screamed.

The boy wheeled and retreated to the corner. He sank to his knees, and the combination hissing and growling sounds intensified. He appeared to be trying to form words, but they were lost in the discordant growls. Just as suddenly the sounds ceased, and Donald began to withdraw, his hands covering his face.

Charla ran to him and turned his face up to hers. What she saw was more serpent than human. The obscene creature's head had round, red, glowing eyes that were partially hidden by a piglike snout. It had yellowed reptilian fangs and a darting tongue. The room was suddenly filled with the choking odor of human excrement.

She screamed and started to back away.

"Leave us alone," the thing hissed. "Go away. Leave us."

Confused and terrified, Charla began backing toward the door. She saw something move behind her and screamed again. It was her aunt who had grabbed her by the arm and was pulling her toward the door.

"My God," Clara muttered, "what is it?"

Donald's body was contorting, writhing back and forth, caught in the agony of accelerated evolution. He was slithering toward them like an enormous, bloated serpent.

Clara recalls that she grabbed her niece, pulled her out into the second floor hallway and slammed the door shut. Charla was hysterical, huddled against the far wall, alternately crying and screaming.

Clara put her arms around Charla who repeated over and over, "That thing, that thing in there is—my son."

Clara says that she held her niece until the panic abated. She kept her own ample body between her niece and the door to Donald's room. On the other side of the barrier the two women could hear the creature slapping its misshapen bulk against the door, guttural cries filling the second floor hallway.

The nightmare lasted for all of ten minutes and was followed by an even more terrifying silence.

Clara described what followed.

"It was a long time before Charla's uncontrollable shaking stopped. When it did, she was so exhausted that she could barely stand up. She was wringing wet with sweat, and I thought she was going to pass out. I left her just long enough to get a damp cloth from the bathroom. I don't know how she did it, but by the time I got back to her, she had somehow found the strength to open the door to Donald's room.

"The boy was lying on the floor, his body all knotted up. I've thought about it since, and I don't see how a human body could be twisted into that shape. You could just tell by the expression on his face that he had been through some terrible kind of agony that we couldn't understand. Other than the way he looked, the only thing I can remember is the sound he was making—it was so strange. Maybe the word is 'primitive.' The other thing I remember is that terrible smell; it almost made me sick.

"Charla was holding him in her arms and crying, but I think the boy was crying even harder.

"Well, you can imagine, even though we had everything in the car, it was several hours before we decided to go ahead and return the stolen items."

In the garage behind the Suffolk County police station, Steinberg finished making an entry in his day log and turned his attention to the young officer Carr had assigned to assist him. Oscar Delvin was 27, a former marine and on loan from the traffic division.

"Let me get this straight, Lieutenant—no intervention?"

"None," Steinberg confirmed, "but you'll have to use your own judgment. All we want you to do is keep an eye on the place. If somebody does show up, make a note of the time and try to get an ident without letting them know you're there."

"What are we looking for?"

Steinberg frowned. "I wish to hell I knew. Something. Anything. Maybe nothing."

Delvin checked the time. It was 10:31 A.M., and he recorded it in his log. Then he crawled into the Ford van borrowed from L.I.P.& L. and backed out of the garage. It would take him approximately 20 minutes to get to 112 Ocean Avenue.

Delvin's log indicates he parked some 30 yards from the house on the opposite side of the street. He positioned himself on the passenger's side where he would not be readily seen.

At 3:13 P.M., a car pulled into the driveway of the house on Ocean Avenue. Three people, two women and a boy, got out of the car. Delvin, using a 35mm camera with a telephoto lens, was able to get pictures of all three. While he watched, one of the women opened the trunk of the car and removed a cardboard box. After some discussion with the other woman, she handed it to the boy. The boy, Delvin recorded, appeared to be reluctant to do whatever it was that the women had requested. Finally the boy relented, and at 3:18 P.M., the boy entered the house carrying the box. The two women waited on the driveway near the rear porch.

Clara Morrison described what happened.

"Charla was very nervous and upset. I did most of the talking, arguing with Donald and instructing him to put each of the items back where he found them. It seemed at the time that most of the belligerence had gone out of him. He was sullen, but he cooperated. I really didn't expect him to be in the house for more than five minutes. I can remember Charla complaining about how cold it was and thinking that it would have been better if we had waited in the car.

"When more than ten minutes passed and Donald didn't come out, Charla turned to me and said, 'Something is wrong.'

" 'You don't think he's trying to make us come in there after him, do you?' I asked her.

"Charla said that was exactly what she was going to do, and she started in."

The two women walked up on the porch and peered into the darkened house.

"Will you just look at that mess?" Clara said. "Just what you would expect from a boy—to be fascinated with a house full of junk. God only knows what has been going on in here since the owners left."

Charla called in to her son, but he did not answer. At that point she was halfway down the hall between the rear entrance and the front room. She called the boy's name repeatedly.

Both women commented on the terrible

odor, and then Charla's aunt motioned her to stop. "I think," she said, "I smell smoke."

Charla agreed. At that point she was standing at the foot of the stairs leading to second floor. "It seems to be coming from up there."

The two women continued to call out for the boy.

When Charla started up the stairs, Clara tried to restrain her. "Don't go up there. What if the place is on fire? You could be trapped."

"But what if Donald is up there and needs help?"

Clara remembers that as her niece started up the stairs, she saw wisps of blue-grey smoke drifting over the top of the stairs. She also recalls that the smoke had a curiously sweet odor about it. She recalls that she was torn between running to the nearest telephone to call the fire department and staying to help her niece find Donald.

Clara was still assessing her options when she heard the door to the rear entrance slam shut. She ran to the door and grabbed the knob but was unable to open it.

While her aunt tried to open the door, Charla ascended the stairs, her eyes fixed on an image that appeared to be materializing out of the smoke. Mingled with the smell of the smoke she realized she smelled a strong perfume as well.

The ill-defined image appeared to be beckoning to her. She recalled thinking that the image was feminine.

By the time she got to the top of the stairs, the

image was gone. When she looked in the bedroom, she saw the reason for the smoke. There was a small vase-like cylinder, and the smoke drifted gently from it. She could hear her aunt calling up to her from the first floor. "What is going on up there? Are you all right? Did you find Donald?"

Charla described what happened then. "For some reason I walked back to the top of the stairs and looked down at my aunt. I wanted to tell her that she shouldn't worry about the smoke. I remember thinking that Donald probably was burning something just to aggravate Clara and me—or scare us. Donald has enjoyed scaring people ever since he was a little boy.

"While I was talking to Clara, I saw her throw her hands up to her face and scream. For some reason I turned around just in time to see this thing screeching toward me. It all happened too fast for me to get a good look at it. It slammed into me, and I was thrown down the stairs. I remember falling and hitting my head and my shoulder. When I landed, I was laying right at Clara's feet. Everything hurt, and I wanted to cry. Just as Clara bent over to help me, something slapped me across the face and grabbed me by the hair. It started dragging me down the hall, and I could hear Clara screaming.

"I was doing everything I could to stop it. I remember thinking, this must be what it's like to be raped. I kicked and screamed and tried to hit it. When it threw the door to the basement open, I managed to get a quick glimpse of all that darkness below me. I even remember that terrible smell. In the background I could hear Clara, screaming and pulling at something. Whatever it was, it was hitting me and kicking me. Finally it shoved me down the steps.

"When I landed at the bottom of the steps, I could taste the blood in my mouth. I was terrified. Every part of me hurt. I couldn't see what it looked like because it was so dark.

"I don't know where Clara was at this point, but I could still hear her screaming. Whatever it was started dragging me across the basement floor. It let go of me, and I could hear sounds, as if it was clawing at something—the walls maybe, I'm not sure.

"Then this panel seemed to peel away, and the thing grabbed me by my hair again and jerked my head up. I was looking into a tiny room, a cell, and it was on fire. There was a sickening smell, like flesh burning. I heard more screams, but this time it wasn't Clara—it was Donald. There was his face right in the middle of that inferno. I tried to reach out to him, tried to claw my way in to help him, but the thing held me back.

"I remember screaming his name—and then I blacked out."

Clara Morrison had her arm around the hysterical woman as she led her back down the driveway toward the car. Despite Steinberg's orders, Delvin jumped out of the L.I.P.& L. van and ran to the woman's assistance.

THE NIGHTMARE CONTINUES

Charla Webster was battered and bleeding from the nose and mouth. Her clothing was torn and dirty. She was so hysterical that she could not tell Officer Delvin or Clara Morrison what had happened for several hours.

When Delvin inquired about the Webster boy, Clara Morrison responded that she did not know where he was.

AUTHOR'S NOTE: WHILE ACCOUNTS OF THIS INCIDENT MAY VARY SLIGHTLY, THERE APPEAR TO BE TWO INCONTROVERTIBLE FACTS. OFFICER DELVIN SAW THREE PEOPLE ENTER THE HOUSE. HE SAW TWO PEOPLE COME OUT. DONALD WEBSTER HAS NOT BEEN SEEN OR HEARD FROM SINCE THAT DAY.

...DAY TWENTY-FOUR...

It was a few minutes after eight o'clock on Friday morning, November 5th, when Officer Oscar Delvin hung up the telephone after his second phone call that morning to the Webster residence. In both instances he had spoken to Clara Morrison, who had returned home with her niece following the incident at the former Difio house the previous day. She reported that her niece had spent a difficult night even though she was under sedation as the result of her injuries. The news about Donald Webster was the same as it had been on the previous call—no word. Delvin looked across the desk at Jerome Steinberg and shook his head. "Nothing," he said, "no phone call, no word, no nothing."

Steinberg had been informed of the Webster boy's disappearance when he returned from the city the previous evening. He had gone immediately to the house on Ocean Avenue, checked it out and interviewed both Clara Morrison and Charla Webster. He had also met with Stephen Carr earlier in the morning to apprise him of the situation. When Delvin indicated that there were no new developments, Steinberg vented his frustration. "Damn it, Oscar, how can an eleven-year-old boy just disappear right under our noses? Three people saw him go into the goddamn house. What the hell happened to him?"

Delvin, not loquacious by nature, had been even more taciturn since the Webster boy had disappeared. He was aware that a strong performance in this case could be his ticket out of the Suffolk County traffic bureau and into a homicide slot. Because of that, he was anxious to look good in the eyes of both Carr and Steinberg. Now, after not being to bed for 26 hours, he was inclined to tell Steinberg that they both would do better with a couple of hours of sleep. Instead, he waited.

Irritated, Steinberg leaned forward with his hands on his desk. "All right, damn it, I guess we don't have any choice. He's been missing for more than twelve hours; we better put out an MPB on him.

"Sara Wine will be in shortly. Let's get her in on this. Have her call Clara Morrison back and

285

get an accurate description of what the boy was wearing when he disappeared. Also, see if she has a recent picture of Donald. Get the vitals: height, weight, color of eyes and hair. Make a note of any unusual scars and habits. The kid was doing pot. See if any of the local pushers have talked to him since five o'clock yesterday. Then send someone over to the school; find out who he ran around with and have somebody talk to all of them. He was pretty tight with the Chambers kid, so he's probably your best lead. He can tell you what the Webster boy talked about, what his interests are, where he likes to hang out, etc."

"Didn't you tell me the Websters were divorced?" Delvin asked. "What about the kid's father? Suppose he hightailed it to his dad's place?"

"Anything is possible," Steinberg said. "Check it out. As soon as we've got a make on him, get it over to the sheriff's department and get it distributed. Fax it to every police department on the island."

"What about the house itself?"

"As soon as we get Sara up to speed we'll go back and check it out one more time. Now that it is daylight again, we might see something we overlooked before."

Delvin left and Steinberg lit a cigarette. He wondered if anyone realized how much he wanted to avoid going back into the house on Ocean Avenue.

* * *

Sara Wine was assigned the responsibility of issuing the MPB on Donald Webster. Her day report for November 5th indicates she went to the Webster household first. She obtained photographs and descriptions of both the boy's physical characteristics and the clothing he was wearing at the time of his disappearance from Mrs. Morrison. She did not talk to or see Charla Webster. In Sara's report on her visit to the Webster house, Steinberg found this comment: "House in disarray, strong odor of alcohol evident."

At Saint Alomar Academy, she spoke to Sister Birdsong and learned that Donald Webster had been expelled the day prior to his disappearance. She then requested and received permission to speak to Lester Chambers. She conducted her interview with Lester in the office formerly occupied by Sister Bertha.

Lester was introduced to Sara and left alone with her. The boy confided to his stepmother later that evening that he was "afraid because I thought she had come to talk to me about the things Kooch and I stole."

Sara did not waste any time getting to the purpose of her visit. "When is the last time you saw Donald Webster?"

Lester had to think. "Day before yesterday in Monsignor McConnell's office."

"The day Donald was expelled?"

Lester nodded.

"Have you talked to him on the telephone since then?"

Lester shook his head. "No, ma'am."

"Do you remember what you two talked about the last time you did talk?"

"Yes, ma'am. We talked about how Sister Bertha died and the stuff from the house being haunted."

Sara paused before she asked the next question. "Are you aware that your friend is missing?"

Lester traced the tip of his finger around the perimeter of the black stain that covered his hand, wrist and forearm and avoided looking at Officer Wine. "Well, I don't know whether he told anyone or not, but he's missing from school because he got expelled."

"Donald never came home last night," Sara said.

Lester looked at the woman in amazement. "You mean he never went home at all? He didn't sleep in his bed or nothing?"

"Did Donald ever talk to you about what kind of problems he was having at home?"

Lester shook his head. He wondered if the officer knew Donald's parents were divorced. Outside of that, he didn't know much about Donald's home life either. Suddenly his face brightened. "His dad has a scrapbook of famous murders."

"Did he ever talk about his father?"

"No, ma'am, just that once."

"What did Donald like to talk about?"

"Mostly he liked to talk about ghosts, things being haunted and getting even with people."

"Did Donald ever say anything to you that would indicate he was thinking about running away?"

Lester thought for awhile. "No, ma'am." The boy's eyes drifted up to the American flag over the blackboard, and she could see Lester mentally counting the stars. She realized that Lester was rapidly becoming bored with the conversation. "If," she said carefully, "Donald did run away, do you think he would go to see his father?"

Lester shrugged. He wasn't big on "ifs" and "supposes." He looked at the woman curiously. "Can I ask you a question?"

Sara nodded. "Certainly."

"Did Kooch run away or something?"

Trained to work with children, Sara answered cautiously. "Yesterday afternoon Donald his mother and her aunt all went back to the house to return some of the items you and Donald had stolen. Donald went into the house and hasn't been seen since."

Lester looked at the woman for several minutes before he asked, "Do you believe in haunted houses, ma'am?"

While Sara Wine conducted her portion of the investigation, Steinberg and Delvin returned to the house on Ocean Avenue. Both men were convinced that a daylight search of the house would reveal something overlooked earlier. They parked in the driveway and checked the perimeter of the property first. Steinberg found footprints but concluded they did not belong to Donald Webster.

They also inspected the garage, the boathouse and the kennel. Other than what Steinberg had observed on previous visits, they found nothing out of the ordinary.

At the rear entrance, Delvin reminded Steinberg of Clara Morrison's story about the door slamming shut and locking. He showed Steinberg the broken lock and demonstrated how easily the door could be opened.

The two men combed the first floor, and when they went upstairs, Steinberg inspected both windows described in the Messato report as being "nailed shut" but which now appeared to open and close easily.

It was while conducting the search of the house on the Friday after the disappearance of Donald Webster that Steinberg came to the realization that most of the phenomena reported by the various witnesses had been seen by more than one witness at a time. Yet each witness gave a different version of what they had seen, felt or heard. During his search of the third floor, he stopped and lit a cigarette.

Delvin asked him, "See anything different, Lieutenant?"

Steinberg shook his head. Later, however, he would tell John Kelly during one of the taping sessions, "In most ways the old house always looked the same and always smelled the same. But the day we went back to look for Donald Webster, I realized that in one way, the old house was different every time we went in it. It never felt the same."

When John Kelly asked him to elaborate, Steinberg couldn't. His only comment was, "Curious, isn't it?"

The two men completed their search of the upper three floors and headed for the basement, pausing just long enough to inventory the items returned by Donald Webster before his disappearance. All of the items were neatly arranged in front of the living room fireplace.

In the basement, Delvin pulled down what remained of the rotted curtains and inspected the windows. Only the window where the boys had first broken into the house afforded access. Delvin assured Steinberg that if Donald had left the house by that window, he would have seen him.

Several minutes later, Delvin paused at the small door under the stairwell. "This is the only place left," he said. "If he isn't in here, we're out of luck."

Delvin pried the door open and looked in. Steinberg was peering over his shoulder.

"Looks like it might have been used to store can goods," Delvin speculated. He was still probing the walls with the beam of his flashlight when he discovered a second access panel at the rear of the small room.

"Eureka," Steinberg said. "Looks like maybe we just found out how Donald Webster got out of here."

Steinberg described how his imagination took off when they discovered the access panel at the rear of that tiny room. "In my mind I could see a tunnel that led out to the bank of the river. All the things I had read about that old house, about the former owners, the nature of the property the house was built on—all started to fall together into a logical explanation."

"Open it up," he told Delvin, aiming his flashlight at the panel. The younger officer peeled the panel away to reveal a small cement room. The stench from the enclosure made them recoil. Instead of an escape, they had discovered a tomb.

Steinberg described what he saw. "I was reasonably certain it was a human skeleton, but it was so small and deformed that I couldn't be certain. It was manacled to the wall by wrist chains. It took me awhile to get my equilibrium. I had never seen a human being deformed to that extent."

Officer Delvin's report described the corpse as having a head that was "more or less oval shaped, with a jaw that looked like it could unhinge." He told Sara Wine, "I kept telling myself you aren't seeing what you think you're seeing, Oscar. There ain't no such thing as a half-human/half-snake."

The two men crawled out of the tiny room gasping for air. Delvin was sick to his stomach. When they managed to get to the first floor,

Steinberg said, "Get on the radio and get the coroner out here."

Dr. George Palmer, representing the Suffolk County coroner's office, arrived at the scene around noon. He was accompanied by a young intern from CCNY. The skeleton was not removed until the coroner had the opportunity to inspect the cell. The manacles were removed by simply slipping the remains through the steel cuffs.

Palmer pointed out several aspects of the tomb to Steinberg. "See this?" he said. "This is decayed fecal material—or what remains of it." He then pointed to a shallow tin tray. "And this, most likely, is what he ate out of."

Palmer carried a small roll of plastic bags. He put the residue of the fecal material in one, scraped the feeding tin and placed residue from that in another, and obtained several hair samples, all of them red and extremely coarse.

By the time they had returned to the first floor, Palmer had begun to speculate. "A couple of things I'm certain about—it was male and it was human. Age? Probably eight, maybe ten years old. I won't be able to pin that down until I've run some tests."

"Something that small can't have been eight to ten years old," Steinberg speculated.

"I've seen them smaller and older," Palmer said. "In case you haven't noticed, Lieutenant, Mother Nature gets ugly every now and then."

"Don't tell me you've run into something like this before?"

"Not personally," Palmer admitted, "but I've read about such cases in journals."

"It's hard for me to believe someone could chain a child up like that."

Palmer shook his head. "Well," he drawled, "the tests will tell us a lot. I can tell you one thing already; he's been there for quite a while. With a little luck we may even get a clue as to why he was there."

A thoroughly upset Steinberg had lit another cigarette. He was pacing back and forth. "Barbaric bastards," he muttered.

"Well, Lieutenant, it wasn't all that many years ago that women were having their babies at home. And just in case you haven't noticed, all babies don't exactly look like the ones on the Gerber baby food jars. Some of them come into this old world looking pretty messed up. I'd venture a guess that is what happened here."

"But why the chains?"

"Lots of reasons—retarded, vicious, mad, maybe all three. It probably never developed because, more than likely, it was too painful or dangerous to confront it with food three times a day. If the truth were known, they were probably hoping the thing would die. Back in those days we didn't have the kinds of institutions we do now. Attitudes change. Back then, an offspring like the one you just found would be a real source of embarrassment to a family."

Steinberg's day log for Friday, November 5th,

reads more like a personal diary than a police log and reveals something about the man. "Delvin and I left the house on Ocean Avenue at 4:38 P.M. Neither of us had much to say on the way back to the station. As tired as I was, I knew I didn't want to go home and try to sleep. I knew this day was going to haunt my nights for a long, long time."

AUTHOR'S NOTE: OF ALL THE MANY STRANGE AND UNUSUAL OCCURRENCES JOHN KELLY RECORDED DURING HIS INVESTIGATION OF THE SECOND AMITYVILLE OCCURRENCE, THE DISCOVERY OF THE REMAINS OF THE DEFORMED CHILD IN THAT TINY, FORGOTTEN, CEMENT CELL SEEMS TO HAVE BOTHERED HIM THE MOST.

AS THE READER KNOWS, THE OPPORTUNITY TO DISCUSS THESE MATTERS WITH JOHN KELLY NEVER MATERIALIZED BECAUSE OF HIS UNTIMELY DEATH. IT SEEMS QUITE APPARENT HOWEVER THAT HE CONSIDERED THE DISCOVERY OF THIS TINY, DEFORMED CORPSE TO BE THE THREAD THAT WOULD LEAD TO THE UNRAVELING OF THE MYSTERY OF THE HOUSE AT 112 OCEAN AVENUE.

DR. PALMER'S REPORT, FILED WITH THE SUFFOLK COUNTY CORONER'S OFFICE, CONFIRMS MOST OF HIS EARLIER SPECULATIONS. THEY BOY WAS NINE YEARS-OLD, AND BONE SAMPLE ANALYSIS DETERMINED THE CAUSE OF DEATH TO BE MALNUTRI-

TION. DEFORMITIES RESULTED, THE RE-
PORT STATES, BOTH AS THE RESULT OF THE
AFOREMENTIONED MALNUTRITION AND
CONGENITAL BIRTH DEFECTS. THE DATE OF
THE CHILD'S DEATH WAS PLACED AT SOME-
WHERE BETWEEN 1890 AND 1900.

JOHN'S RESEARCH INTO THIS MATTER
INDICATES THAT THERE HAD BEEN THREE
AND POSSIBLY MORE DIFFERENT STRUC-
TURES ON THE SAME SITE. HE WAS NOT
ABLE TO DETERMINE WHETHER OR NOT
ANY OF THE SUBSEQUENT STRUCTURES IN-
CORPORATED PARTS OF THE PREVIOUS
BUILDINGS. JOHN'S NOTES ALSO INDICATE
THAT ON AT LEAST TWO OCCASIONS, THE
STRUCTURES ON THAT SITE SAT VACANT
FOR PROLONGED PERIODS OF TIME. THIS
LATTER FACT PROBABLY ALLOWED JOHN TO
SPECULATE ABOUT SOMEONE USING OR
LIVING IN THE STRUCTURE WHILE IT WAS
ABANDONED.

. . . DAY TWENTY-FIVE . . .

At noon on Saturday, November 6th, Lt. Jerome Steinberg called his team together in his office at the Suffolk County Police Department. The purpose of the meeting was to update Captain Stephen Carr.

The Steinberg team now included both Sara Wine, on loan from the Suffolk County School Corporation, and Officer Oscar Delvin, on loan from the Traffic Division. By the time Stephen Carr arrived, he had read all of the reports relating to both Bellini and Webster as well as the update on the Leon Silverman case. Carr opened the meeting with a brief speech.

"I know you're all tired, and I know you're as disappointed as I am by our lack of progress.

297

Sooner or later though, we'll get a break, so stick with it." He looked at Sara Wine. "Start us off, Sara. Where do we stand on Donald Webster?"

"The Webster boy has been missing since Thursday afternoon. We waited until Friday morning to issue an MPB. Clara Morrison gave me a current photograph and updated the statistics. The flyers have been printed and distributed to the local merchants and service clubs. Late yesterday afternoon I finally got in touch with the boy's father. He hasn't heard from Donald either. From what the Morrison woman tells me, I would be surprised if he did try to contact his father. Apparently they didn't get along all that well."

"What about his school?"

"I've been over to Saint Alomar twice. They know the situation. In addition, I talked to the Chambers boy. I'm convinced he doesn't know where Donald is either."

Carr turned to Delvin. "What have you got?"

"I took Jerry's suggestion and ran the ladies through the traps a second time—same stories, same discrepancies. Nothing new there."

Carr was slumped in his chair. "When I first heard about this, I was convinced the Webster boy had taken off, and I thought it would be just a matter of time until he got cold and hungry enough to come home. Now I'm not so certain. Did you check with any other sources?"

"I checked with two of the better locals. They

said they never heard of him. Another claims the kid bought an occasional joint from a guy by the name of Moe Williams. I haven't had any luck locating him either."

Carr looked at Steinberg. "Do you know this guy, Williams?"

Steinberg nodded. "Runs more of a small-time bunco operation than anything else. The last time he was hauled in he was nailed for selling the kids chic weed and passing it off as grass."

"The kids didn't know the difference?" Delvin grinned.

"I wouldn't," Steinberg admitted.

"I just finished reading Oscar's report," Sara interjected. "I know this sounds far-fetched, but is there any possibility that Donald Webster is still hiding somewhere in that house?"

Steinberg, unshaven and obviously weary, leaned forward with his arms on Carr's desk. "Like I told Oscar, anything is possible. We went over that damn place from top to bottom yesterday before we stumbled across the body in that room under the basement stairs. I suppose its possible that there is another hidden room somewhere else in that old dump."

"Is it worth pursuing?" Carr asked.

"I got a gut feeling that says it's a waste of time," Steinberg admitted. "But it's an option."

Carr's face was cast in a frown. "Why is it that everything ties back to that damned house and yet none of it makes any sense? I think we better take a look at how we're approaching this whole thing. We've got to ask ourselves why it is we aren't making any progress. Are we looking in the right places? Are we asking the right questions? Then ask yourself, how the hell can something like this happen? We've got an officer stationed right across the street; he can see both entrances. He sees three people enter the house and two people come out. He stays on the scene until he gets backup, and when he investigates, he finds nothing. Not only that, we've got two decidedly different versions of what went on in that house while the two women were in there. None of this makes any sense."

"What about Dr. Palmer's report?" Delvin asked.

"No surprises," Steinberg said. "I stopped by his office this morning and picked up a copy of his report. Palmer believes the boy's body has been down there ninety, maybe a hundred years. He said if we tried to pin him down, he'd say the child died somewhere around the turn of century, give or take five years either way."

"Couldn't have been," Delvin protested. "That house is old, but it hasn't been there that long."

"The current house could have been built right over the previous one or right on top of the previous foundation. Palmer thinks there are any number of ways it could have happened."

"So, given all of that, what is our next step?" Sara asked.

"That is the problem. There isn't any obvious next step," Carr said. "We keep digging and picking until something breaks. I've been in this game too long; something will pop up." He looked around the room. "Okay, so much for Webster; what about Bellini? Anything new?"

Steinberg shook his head. "Nothing. No trace of him; no trace of the woman he was supposedly seeing. One thing is curious about these two cases though; they both came up missing at the same house, and they both seem to end right there."

"And they both happened in broad daylight," Sara added.

"Alright," Carr sighed. He leaned back, put his hands behind his head and closed his eyes. It was his standard way of letting them know that the meeting was over. As the trio filed from his office, he asked Steinberg to wait. "On the way into the office this morning, I got to wondering —has Sara been able to dig up anything on Chambers and his first wife?"

"She was working on it until this Donald Webster thing popped up, but no real break through so far."

"Don't let go of it," Carr advised.

Steinberg shoved his hands in his pockets and nodded. "Know something, Stephen? At the moment I feel like a juggler with one too many balls in the air."

"Tell me about it," Carr smiled.

* * *

That evening, Alice Chambers retired to her button room, took down her journal and began to write:

"Last night, the vision came to me again. She held out her hands to me, but this time there was no creature for me to shun. Has the burden been lifted from her?"

. . . DAY TWENTY-SIX . . .

In reflecting on the second Amityville occurrence, Jerome Steinberg would tell John Kelly that it was one of the most difficult periods of his life. "Never," he stated, "has any one series of events so troubled me. Even more disconcerting was the feeling, when everything was finally culminated, that there was little I could have done to alter the course of events."

It was Sunday morning, November 7th, and Steinberg, again unable to sleep, had been up for several hours. He spent the early hours of the morning reviewing his notes, plodding through his day logs and resketching his matrix of events. His conclusion was the same; the convoluted series of events was totally illogical and unrelated. Yet he knew the opposite was true. There was no logic, and if there was no logic, a course of action was hard to identify. Still, perhaps from years of experience, he knew that the answer was somehow contained in the house at 112 Ocean Avenue.

By midmorning he had reached the point of frustration. Even while plowing through the voluminous edition of the *Sunday Times*, his mind kept returning to the house in Amityville.

At ten, he showered, shaved and prepared to go down the street to Rico's, a restaurant where he enjoyed the Sunday morning brunch. As he was leaving the apartment, his phone rang. It was Stephen Carr.

"Did I wake you?"

"I was just on my way out the door to get some breakfast. What's up?"

"We just got home from church. On the way home I was telling the little lady how rough the past couple of weeks have been and she said I should invite you over for some chicken and dumplings. She thought a little home cooking might change your outlook on life."

"Couldn't hurt," Steinberg said. "How soon?"

"Whenever—we'll eat around noon. I've already got a fire in the fireplace."

"Within the hour," Steinberg said. At the last minute he decided to take his Amityville file with him in case Carr wanted to talk. At that point, he had no way of knowing that he would not have the opportunity to return to his apartment for almost 48 hours.

By the time Roy Chambers had driven his family home following the nine o'clock Mass, he was livid. He had learned about the missing Webster boy from an announcement in the church bulletin. On the way home, he interrogated his son about Donald Webster.

Lester answered all of his father's questions. He held nothing back and did not attempt to hide the truth. In doing so, Roy, for the first time, learned about the series of thefts from the house on Ocean Avenue.

Learning that his son was guilty of theft was more than Roy could handle. By the time he had parked the car and gone into the house, he was in a rage. Alice May's diary entry says simply but eloquently, "His behavior bordered on hysteria."

Both Lester and Ellen were sent to their rooms. In the couple's bedroom, Roy turned his wrath on his wife. "How long have you known about all of this?" he shouted.

Alice had seen her husband lose his temper on several occasions, but she had never seen him act like this. When her answers faltered and she was unable to remember specific details, he accused her of lying in an attempt to cover for the boy.

"That boy has been nothing but trouble since day one," he fumed.

Alice was terrified, both at her husband's irrational display of temper and his threats of bodily harm. The more Chambers gestured, threatened and shouted, the more the woman withdrew into a shell. Even when she knew the answer and tried to respond, her mouth was too dry and she was unable to speak. She was, she wrote in her journal, "unable to think straight."

In another entry, she called him an "animal" and wrote, "He shed his repressions and stripped me of my self-respect." She did not, probably because she was too embarrassed, detail the severity or duration of her beating. However she did record in detail the nature of her cuts and bruises. She would not know for several days, and then only after seeing a doctor, that the excessive swelling in her left arm and hand was the result of a broken wrist, caused by her husband throwing her over the end of the bed and up against the wall. The same blow apparently dislodged two teeth, one of which she swallowed in her attempt to stifle her scream.

Alice May wrote:

"I was spitting up blood. It was difficult to breath. I put my fingers in my mouth and felt the jagged edge of my broken teeth. When I coughed, I realized that I had swallowed one of the broken teeth."

It was in the early afternoon that Alice May succeeded in escaping her husband's wrath and managed to find sanctuary in her button room. Her journal entry begins:

> *"He is furious with both the boy and me. So far he has only taken his anger out on me. He has not yet touched the boy. I feared for my life. I have never seen such rage. I do not think he quit beating me because he thinks I have suffered enough. I believe he quit because he is too exhausted to continue."*

Another entry, obviously written with a great deal of anguish and pain, described how Roy Chambers turned his unbridled rage on his son. The distraught Alice May wrote that she could hear the boy "begging for mercy." This was written about a boy who had learned that expressions of pain displeased his father and who had accepted his earlier punishments in stoic silence. Later, when Alice May was allowed to go to the boy and comfort him, she found him sobbing and covered with blood.

Although Alice does not specifically state that her husband used the belt on Lester, she does refer to "that awful belt."

In the Carr household, several miles away from where the Chambers tragedy was unfolding, Steinberg and Carr watched the second game of a CBS National Football League doubleheader. Two of the four Carr boys were preparing to leave for a late Sunday afternoon youth group meeting at the First Presbyterian

Church of Glencoe. Sue Carr had managed to get the two younger boys to retire to their room to study.

Carr waited until the two men were alone before stoking the fire and turning off the television. Without looking at Steinberg, he asked. "Okay, let's have it. There was a whole lot you weren't saying yesterday at the meeting. What do you think happened to the Webster kid?"

"Who knows, Stephen? Maybe he ran away. Maybe he's hiding somewhere in the house. Or maybe that damn house ate him." Steinberg tried to sound light about the subject.

"I'm serious."

"So am I, Stephen. I'm the first to admit that I'm as baffled by all of this as I've been by anything I ever tackled."

"What about Delvin? Do you think he went to sleep on the job? Wasn't he paying attention or what?"

"I suppose he could have dropped the ball, but I don't think so. He knows you've got a homicide slot open, and he's trying pretty hard to impress you."

"Could he have just plain missed him? After all, the weather wasn't all that good."

"It wasn't that bad either. Cold, windy, overcast—but there was nothing wrong with the visibility."

"What about Charla Webster?"

Steinberg sighed. "Now there's one screwed-up lady, Stephen, but maybe I'd be screwed up, too, if I'd been through everything she's been through. If you're asking me if I think she made any of this up, the answer is 'no.' You've been in that house—there's something different about it."

Carr was still crouched in front of the fireplace. "After you left yesterday, I reread your report a couple of times and called Sam Carter. Sam headed up the last investigation over there the last time things boiled up. I told him the Webster woman claimed she saw a vision of an old woman."

"Did you tell him you and I saw the same old woman?"

"I haven't had the guts to tell anyone what we saw that first day," Carr admitted. "Anyway, Carter said he wasn't surprised at anything people told him about that old house. He said he had seen a couple of things ten years ago that he still hadn't told anyone about."

Steinberg took out a cigarette and played with it. "You know what Charla Webster thinks? She thinks her son followed that old woman right into the fire."

"That would be the same fire we saw and Lomax couldn't find a trace of," Carr reminded him.

Steinberg stood up and leaned against the mantle of the fireplace. Through the window he could see the snow falling. "It doesn't sound very damn professional, Stephen, or very reassuring—but I don't know where to go for help. If you were to ask me what my next step is, I'd have to tell you I don't know."

Carr grunted. "I could give you a pep talk, but who would give me one?"

"What we need is some breaks. We need a break in the Silverman case, the Bellini case and now the Webster case."

"We're looking at this thing too logically. We keep trying to tie these cases one to the other."

Steinberg held up his hand with his fingers spread. He counted them off. "Okay, first we've got Bellini, then comes Silverman. Then we go to Jacalyn Cordes. Then the Messato couple and now the Webster kid. And that's just the ones we know about. The spooky thing, Stephen, is that in one way or another, every damn one of those cases I've just counted off is somehow con- nected to that house on Ocean Avenue."

Stephen Carr moved a little closer to the fire and shuddered. "I know it, damn it, I know it."

In another part of town, Clara Morrison ar- rived at her niece's house after visiting the gravesite of Jacalyn Cordes in nearby Glen Ha- ven. Clara had talked to Charla earlier in the day, and Charla was expecting her. Neverthe- less, when she arrived, the house was dark. She entered, called out to her niece but received no answer. Clara recalls that she thought she heard water running in a second floor bathroom. Thinking her niece might be taking a bath and had not heard her call out to her, she went upstairs. She found Charla in the bathtub. The taps were turned on full force with the water spilling out over the rim of the tub. The cascading water was sickly pink in color. Charla had tried to commit suicide by slitting her wrists.

Clara was able to get her niece out of the tub and call 911. Her prompt action saved Charla Webster's life.

By nightfall, a battered Alice Chambers had set her journals aside and watched the clock nervously. She had been in her button room for several hours. Roy Chambers seldom retired before ten o'clock, but when she heard the bedroom door close at a few minutes after eight, she breathed a sigh of relief. Roy seldom went into the bedroom unless he was changing clothes or preparing to retire. She opened her journal, made note of the time and scribbled, "I know that it is nearly over." Those seven words would come back to haunt Alice.

The journal entry would lead us to believe that Alice thought the long and difficult day was finally over. In view of what transpired that evening, the entry is subject to other interpretations.

She went to her son's room and found him sobbing and restless, still wearing the compresses she had designed to cover his network of cuts and welts.

"Are you all right?" she whispered.

Lester nodded without speaking.

Alice May encouraged the boy to get under the

covers. "It is very cold outside. You'll catch a chill before morning."

Lester complied, and his stepmother bent over and kissed him on the forehead. When she did, she felt the blood seep from her own split lips. In her diary she said, "I remember the pain and thinking I would be sick from the salty, hot taste."

"Things will get better," she promised the boy as she turned out the lights.

She left the boy's room and looked in briefly on his sister. Ellen had gone to sleep with the lights on. She turned them off, went briefly to her button room and then into the couple's bedroom. She believed her husband would be sleeping.

THE EVENTS THAT TRANSPIRED IN THE CHAMBERS' BEDROOM THE NIGHT OF NOVEMBER 7TH ARE KNOWN ONLY TO ALICE CHAMBERS. HER JOURNAL IS THE ONLY RECORD. THE FOLLOWING IS A WORD-FOR-WORD TRANSCRIPT:

"He had been in the bedroom long enough that I dared to hope he was already asleep. When I opened the door, he was sitting in the bed, wearing his pajamas and reading from the Bible. He did not look up at me, nor did he acknowledge the fact that I was in the room. I could believe, from his actions, that he was still very much agitated with me.

"I chose to change to my gown in the room

across the hall rather than reveal myself to him. I did not think I could stand any further abuse or humiliation.

"When I returned to the bedroom in my nightgown and robe, he glared at me. His expression betrayed his anger and hostility. When he finally spoke, his tone was rancorous. 'How could you deceive me?' he said.

"I wanted to tell him that I never did intend to deceive him. I wanted to say that because I myself had lived so close to Lester's misdeeds, I somehow believed that he understood what was happening. But I did not say that—and whatever I did say was inadequate. He would not listen, and my apology fell on deaf ears.

" 'A woman who will not stand by her husband has no place in this house that I have dedicated to God.'

"I inquired as to how I could regain his trust, and he looked at me with contempt. He did not answer me. Instead he placed the Bible on the nightstand and appeared as though he would get out of bed. For a moment I feared that he would assault me again, but he turned his back on me and rolled over in preparation for sleep.

" 'Get in bed,' he demanded and turned out the light.

"I groped for the edge of the bed in the darkness. I remember praying that this terrible day would end without further incident. As I crawled into bed I felt him recoil and

draw further away from me. He lay motionless, and I pulled the covers up to my face. I
could tell that he was not yet asleep, and I
began to pray. My eyes were shut against the
hate I felt.

"After a short while his breathing regulated
and I believed him to be asleep. Only then did
I cease my prayers and open my eyes.

"She was there.

"How do I describe this unfathomable
nightmare?

"I could sense her presence.

"I could feel her coldness.

"I could smell her perfume.

"Then I saw the birthing repeated.

"The thing-child was emerging. It was
there in the room with me—the countenance of evil, the personification of all that is
vile, a thing which exudes the inevitability of
decay. Guttural sounds emanated from its
throat. There were cackles of derision. It was
consummate depravity, a demonic force.
The skin was like parchment, revoltingly
transparent, revealing the poisons coursing
through its veins.

"My husband did not move, yet I knew he
had awakened and was watching.

"The thing-child was evolving into a
clawed, two-headed serpent, a monstrosity
with burning red eyes and a darting forked
tongue. Its eyes seared my soul. It hissed in
defiance as it slithered up on the bed. Somehow it held the belt my son had stolen. It

made the object taut and moved menacingly toward us.

"Its course was irrevocable.

"I wanted to scream, but there was no sound.

"I do not think my husband realized its intent. It moved mindlessly toward him, trailing excrement in its wake.

"Slowly it began to coil around my husband's foot, and then it encompassed his legs. Why did he not cry out? There were no sounds to accompany his terror.

"I cannot, even now as I dwell upon what I have witnessed, describe this terrible thing.

"From my husband's legs, it moved up until it encircled his body. I could see it tightening. I could hear the evidence of his pain. Bones shattered. Flesh tore away. It encircled his throat and searched out his mouth. His face, at first flushed with silent panic, began to drain of color. He was gasping for air. The searching, probing tentacle of the belt pried open his mouth and tore out his tongue.

"His scream was silenced.

"I could but watch.

"The skin covering his face began to split and shred. Fluids, crimson-black, steaming and thick, erupted from his head, and a muted half-animal cry escaped from him. Blood disgorged from his mouth and ears, even from the sockets of his bulging eyes.

"There was one final scream. I do not

know whether it was my husband surrendering to death or the thing-creature trumpeting its triumph.

"I was awash in pooling and congealing blood, an island amidst unspeakable carnage. The thing-child slithered back and forth in the human debris, again set upon its metamorphic journey.

"I reached out and pulled the belt from the detritus. Then I cast it aside.

"The door burst open, and I saw the boy standing there, horrified, a scream of unbridled terror slowly building in his throat.

"He stumbled blindly toward the bed.

"I pleaded with him to get help. He looked at me and at the carnage in the middle of the bed. Then he fled."

The interrogation of Alice May Chambers and her stepson lasted far into the night. The story they would repeat over and over defied belief. It was, Stephen Carr would say, the most incredible story he had ever heard.

Alice carefully described over and over the highly improbable scene in which a woman gave birth to a two-headed serpent that ultimately coiled around her husband and crushed him to death. The boy, to Carr's astonishment, corroborated every word.

Carr had arrived at the scene in the Chambers house shortly after midnight. About the body in the Chambers bedroom, he said, "If the man's wife and the boy hadn't given us an identification, I don't know how long it would have taken us to establish the identity of the victim."

Following Carr's arrival on the scene, Monsignor McConnell arrived to administer the sacrament of Extreme Unction.

...DAY TWENTY-SEVEN...

Steinberg emerged from a tangle of covers and picked up the telephone. For the first time in two weeks he had slept through the night. "Steinberg," he finally managed.

"Awake yet?" Carr asked.

"Not yet. Give me a second." With the receiver clenched between his shoulder and ear, he rubbed his eyes and tried to get his bearing. "Go ahead, Stephen."

"Are you sitting down?"

"Actually I'm still in bed. What's up?"

"We logged a call last night at ten. The kid said his dad had just been killed by a big snake."

"A snake? I'm glad you're handling it. I hate snakes." There was a lightness in Steinberg's voice that hadn't been there in weeks.

"I hate to rain on your parade, Jerry, but I think you better get involved with this one. Roy Chambers is dead."

"Lester Chambers' father?"

"That's the one. I'm home now changing clothes. I've been over there all night, and now I'm headed back. I'll pick you up in fifteen minutes."

Steinberg hung up and started to get out of bed. "Shit," he muttered to himself, "the day hasn't even started and already I feel lousy."

Steinberg stood in the heated vestibule of his apartment complex while he waited. The streets were coated with a thin veneer of ice and the barren tree branches in the park across the street sagged under the added weight. It was 7:41 A.M., November 8th.

When Carr arrived, his grey police car was coated with the same thin coating of ice. He inched his way to the curb, and Steinberg got in.

"There's coffee in the thermos. It's stronger than bull's breath, but it will wake you up."

While Steinberg unscrewed the lid and poured a cup, Carr updated him. "Lattimore was working the desk last night when the call came in. At first he couldn't tell whether it was a boy or girl. Finally he got the kid to settle down enough to figure out what he was saying."

"What's this about a snake?"

"It's all on tape. I duped it off the monitor

319

line. The insurance company will want a copy of it anyway."

Steinberg punched the play button. There were several seconds of static and screeching before Lester's voice came through.

"My—my dad has—has been killed. My stepmother—she's screamin'—"

"Who is this?" he could hear Lattimore demand.

"He—he's dead."

"All right, I understand." Lattimore's voice was calm and reassuring. "But you'll have to identify yourself. Now, very slowly, give me your name and address."

"He—he ain't breathin'. He—he's all broken up, layin'—layin' in the middle of his bed. There's blood—lots of blood."

"Give me your name," Lattimore repeated.

The voice shattered into hysterical sobs. There were shouts and screams in the background. Steinberg stopped the tape, rewound it and played it a second time.

Carr reached over and shut off the machine. "Heard enough? The dispatcher took it from there. Delvin made the run. Then he called me. I got there just before midnight. When I got there, Chambers' wife was still hysterical. She insisted on staying in the room where the body was. She looks like a goddamn truck hit her—cuts and bruises all over her. The boy doesn't look much better."

Steinberg looked out the window. "What's this about a snake?"

"Same old bizarre shit that's plagued us from the beginning. Alice Chambers claims she and her husband had just gone to bed when she heard a noise in the room. She said she saw an old woman standing at the foot of the bed, and she was carrying something. Then she started clawing at her stomach, and a snake popped out. Then she said the snake crawled up on the bed, coiled around her husband, and that was that."

"Cause of death?"

"The coroner was still there when I went home to get cleaned up, but from the looks of Chambers it could be anything from asphyxiation to massive internal injuries. It's a mess, Jerry. You think you've seen everything, and then you run into something like this."

Steinberg took a sip of coffee. "Old woman, huh? Sound familiar?"

Carr chewed on his lower lip. "I was hoping you wouldn't bring it up."

When Carr and Steinberg pulled into the Chambers driveway, they could see people milling around inside the house. A converted maroon mini-van was parked at the curb, and the body of Roy Chambers, concealed in a drab, grey-green, plastic bag on a gurney was being loaded by two men.

In the living room, Steinberg introduced Stephen Carr to Monsignor McConnell. A woman from the church, called in by McConnell, moved quietly about the house, serving coffee and consoling the children.

"What about the kids?" Steinberg asked.

The woman informed him that Roy Chambers' sister was flying in from Buffalo. She was expected to arrive around noon. After talking to the woman, Steinberg moved through the house, noting the surroundings and appointments more carefully than he had on previous visits. He took special note of the large number of religious artifacts and icons throughout the house.

In the kitchen he found Ellen Chambers, her face swollen and puffy. The girl was still crying, and Steinberg decided to talk to her later.

In the living room he inquired about Alice Chambers. He was told the family doctor had been called in. She had been given a sedative, put to bed and was finally asleep.

"How long before we can talk to her?"

McConnell informed him that the doctor said the woman would sleep for several hours.

He caught up with Carr in the second floor bedroom where Roy Chambers had died. Delvin was still there and assured Steinberg that the room hadn't been touched other than to remove the body. Standing at the foot of the bed, Carr went over the details once again.

"—then she described how the belt turned into a snake, crawled up his leg, eventually wrapped itself around the entire body and crushed him." Finished, Carr folded his arms and waited. Steinberg lit a cigarette.

"What do you think, Jerry?"

Steinberg exhaled a cloud of smoke and

watched it drift in the air over Carr's head. "Well, the first thing that comes to mind is—it would take a hell of a lot of strength to bust up a body the way you and Delvin describe Chambers. I couldn't do it, and I'm a hell of a lot bigger than Alice Chambers. I guess the question is, do you think she killed him?"

"Come on, Jerry. From what those kids tell me, the guy was pounding on her all day. Sounds to me like she had all the motive she needed."

"If she did do it," Delvin interjected, "she did it one-handed. Her left wrist is all swollen up. Looks to me like it's broken. She's supposed to go down and have x-rays taken when she gets up."

"Maybe she had help," Carr suggested.

"Like who? The kids?"

Carr grunted. "Very funny." He wandered aimlessly around the room, studying the blood-soaked bedding, the belt on the floor beside the bed, and the picture of Alice Chambers on the bureau. "Every time I look at that damned picture she seems to get smaller, and I think it's less and less likely she did it."

"Have you talked to the boy?" Steinberg asked.

Carr nodded. "I had him take me through it from start to finish. It meshes exactly with what his stepmother told me."

Fathers Chiraldi and Cannon arrived at the house on 112 Ocean Avenue shortly after noon.

They parked in the driveway and checked out the exterior buildings before entering the house. Cannon carried the authority to conduct the Church's investigation in his pocket. It was signed by Bishop Lawrence Markland.

The two men entered the house through the rear door and systematically worked their way through every room on the first floor. Then they compared notes. Neither man felt he had seen or encountered anything extraordinary.

On the second floor they inspected the charred area where the small vial had been left burning and then proceeded to the third floor. While Chiraldi watched and recorded, Cannon inspected every window, closet and recessed area.

"What do you think?" Chiraldi finally asked.

"I think," Cannon hesitated, "something must be very different. It's not at all what I expected to find."

"No sense of an influence?"

"Not so far."

The two men proceeded to the basement, again poking the beams of their flashlights into every corner. They culminated their search with an inspection of the small room under the stairs where the skeleton of the child had been discovered. Cannon inspected the manacles, looked at Chiraldi and shook his head.

As they stood in the darkness, Chiraldi said, "Curious, isn't it? Instead of hostility, I almost get a sense of tranquility."

"Or emptiness," Cannon countered. "I don't

doubt that they experienced an influence here, but whatever it was, it's not active now. Maybe it has something to do with the body of the child they found under the stairwell."

"This so-called tranquility comes a little late, doesn't it?" Chiraldi sighed.

Cannon started toward the rear door. "A little late for some, yes, but for others, perhaps just in time."

Chiraldi understood.

In his office after lunch, Steinberg called Sara Wine at her office at the Suffolk County School Corporation on Cressmar Street.

"Sara, it's Jerry. I've got a note here to call you. Did you come up with something on the Webster boy?"

Sara hesitated. "Nothing on the boy, but I stopped by the Webster house on the way to work this morning and Mrs. Morrison told me Charla Webster tried to commit suicide last night. She's in critical condition at St. Vincent Hospital."

"Will she make it?"

"Touch and go, but they think so."

Steinberg sagged back in his chair and closed his eyes.

That night, Teresa Chambers Mercer, Roy Chambers' sister, moved Ellen and Lester into a motel on Montgomery Street. She thought it best that the children not spend another night in the house where their mother had committed suicide and their father was murdered. She informed authorities that she would return the following morning to be certain that the children had enough clothing to tide them through the funeral.

Mrs. Mercer was in a quandary. Neither Ellen nor Lester seemed particularly close to their stepmother, and in her mind there was a very real issue of who was responsible for the children's welfare. Furthermore, Alice Chambers appeared to be very unstable. Monsignor McConnell had confirmed as much in a conversation earlier in the day.

After conversations with both Saint Alomar and Saint Agnes officials and two lengthy long-distance conversations with her husband in Buffalo, Mrs. Mercer decided that the children would return with her to Buffalo.

As she prepared Ellen and Lester for bed that evening, she examined the discoloration on Lester's hand.

"What is this?" she asked.

Lester shrugged and explained that he had been to two different doctors. He also mentioned that in the last day or so it had started to go away.

Late that same evening, Sister Carla Birdsong stepped from the Greyhound bus that delivered her back to Glencoe after a three-day holiday with her mother in Camden, New Jersey. Sister Carla was not wearing her habit.

As she stepped from the warmth of the terminal to look for a taxi, she saw a man step from his car and disappear into an all-night drugstore.

Sister Carla was certain she recognized the man.

The man, wearing a leather jacket with the collar pulled up high around his throat, came out of the store and got back in his car. As he did, Sister Carla called out to him.

"Father Bellini?"

The man looked up momentarily, did not respond—and drove away.

. . . DAY TWENTY-EIGHT . . .

Steinberg was in Carr's cruiser on the morning of Tuesday, November 9th, heading east on Montgomery Street. It was a dismal, gray morning with a bone-chilling wind out of the southwest. Their prospects for the day were unpleasant, their mission even more so. They rode in silence.

At 9:57 A.M., Carr pulled up to the curb in front of the house at 3257 Oak Street and delayed just long enough to extract an oversized cream-colored envelope from his briefcase.

The two men stepped from the car, threaded their way past patches of ice on the sidewalk and went up on the porch. Steinberg rang the doorbell. Alice Chambers came to the door. Her face was hollow and gaunt, her eyes bloodshot and swollen. Her left arm was in a sling, and there was a cast on her arm. She held onto the door for support.

"I have a warrant for your arrest," Steinberg said. "You are charged with the murder of your husband, Roy M. Chambers."

. . . EPILOGUE . . .

For all intents and purposes, the Second Amityville Occurrence ended with the arrest of Alice Chambers. John Kelly's files seem to indicate that the death of Roy Chambers was the concluding event.

Still there are questions.

What really happened?

A noted psychic, Dr. Arnold Spencer Freeman, advances some rather interesting theories.

Alice May Chambers, Freeman believes, was a sensitive of the highest order. She was spiritually synchronous with the restless soul in the house at 112 Ocean Avenue. Freeman further believes that the recurring vision of the sorrowful old woman to a wide variety of people proves how desperate she was to free herself from her awful burden.

Freeman had another interesting theory about Alice Chambers. He claims that it was her religious conviction that made her both receptive and vulnerable. Freeman goes on to say that the bond between the two women and their frequent communication through sympathetic non-verbal transfer (dreams) would not have materialized if Alice Chambers had not held such strong religious convictions. Freeman maintains that individuals with this conviction already acknowledge the existence of the other realm (souls, purgatory, heaven, hell, etc) and as such, make themselves available for dialogue with the spiritual dimension.

Freeman interprets the restless soul to be the mother of the deformed child-thing whose body was found in the tiny room hidden under the stairs leading to the basement. According to Freeman, he believes that the restless soul carried the burden of two sins. One, she had given birth to a demon. Second, believing that the deformed child was a demon, she chained it in that room and permitted it to die. Freeman doubts if the child-thing was a demon at birth but believes that it evolved into one. He said, "You can provoke any dog into becoming mean by being cruel to it." At any rate, knowing that she was responsible for this demon, the woman felt compelled to isolate it and protect us from it. Much of the hostility felt by people who entered the house was simply the restless soul warning them about the demon. The shredding away of her skin was indeed a symbolic birthing or a confession of her sin.

The child-thing simply wanted out. It wanted to be free of its near-century of incarceration—and it could not leave its tiny cell until it manipulated Donald Webster into replacing it.

Donald Webster was nothing more than an unfortunate pawn in this struggle. Freeman is convinced that when Donald Webster entered that house the last time, he exchanged places with the child-thing. The demon had the power to manipulate the Webster boy—and did.

Freeman went on to say that the disappearance of Donald Webster into the other realm should not be difficult to accept. Thousands and thousands of individuals disappear every year; the majority are never seen or heard from again.

Well, so much for the views of Dr. Arnold Freeman, and so much for the content of the Kelly files and tapes.

Did John Kelly see in this bizarre tangle of events a thread of connection that does not exist? Or did he happen upon a moment in time and space when the other realm had its way with us?

There were, as the reader would suspect, frequent contacts with Kristen Kelly, John's widow, during the course of this project. As the project neared its inevitable end, I called Kristen to inquire what she wanted done with

John's files. She asked that they be returned to her.

On the first day of November, two years ago, I carefully packaged and mailed John's files: interview tapes, copies of logs, journals, newspaper articles, weather records and Alice Chambers' disturbing diary.

The package never arrived.

Finally there is the matter of the people involved.

Monsignor David McConnell . . . was relieved of his clerical and administrative responsibilities when Saint Alomar Academy was closed because of declining enrollment. David McConnell died of a heart attack, September 22, 1988.

Lester Chambers . . . completed his schooling in Buffalo, NY. The strange discoloration that plagued him from the time he entered the house on Ocean Avenue began to dissipate shortly after the death of his father.

Ellen Chambers . . . completed her schooling in Buffalo. She is married and has one child.

Stephen Carr . . . retired, whereabouts unknown.

Sara Wine . . . remarried, retired, whereabouts unknown.

Father Vincent Chiraldi . . . returned to school to further his studies. He now teaches at a large midwestern Catholic University.

Father William Cannon . . . is confined to a wheelchair as a result of a traffic accident. He lives in retirement on Long Island.

Charla Webster . . . recovered from her self-inflicted wounds. She remarried in 1987 and now lives in England.

Clara Morrison . . . died in 1988 after a prolonged illness.

Virginia Heart . . . retired when Saint Alomar was closed. Whereabouts unknown.

Father Joseph Bellini . . . whereabouts unknown.

Donald "Kooch" Webster . . . entered the house at 112 Ocean Avenue on the afternoon of Friday, November 5th. Donald Webster has not been seen or heard from since that time.

Jerome Steinberg . . . resigned from the Suffolk County Police Department six weeks to the day after the arrest of Alice Chambers. He served in the capacity of *amicus curiae* (friend of the court) in the two court hearings surrounding the death of Roy Chambers.

Steinberg's untimely resignation means that two questions peripheral to the second Amityville occurrence were left unanswered. The investigation into/the death of Monica Chambers never materialized. Did Monica Chambers commit suicide, or did her husband administer the overdose of barbiturates? Secondly, was Monsignor David McConnell aware of what really happened but restricted by his vows from sharing that information with the authorities? Of lesser importance, had Father Joseph Bellini revealed the nature of his relationship with the young woman about whom very little is known?

And finally, Alice May Chambers, charged with the murder of Roy M. Chambers, was never brought to trial.

In June of the year following her husband's bizarre death, Alice Chambers was turned over to the New York State Correctional Board and underwent extensive psychiatric evaluation. Following those examinations she was assigned to an institution for the criminally insane. She is still incarcerated.

John Kelly visited Alice Chambers on two occasions. She had no recollection of the events that transpired during the 28-day period. She does not remember Roy, Lester or Ellen Chambers. She is still, she maintains, a member of the Order of the Poor Handmaids.

In the spring of 1990, Alice Chambers' second book of poetry was published. It is entitled *The Meaning Of Winter*.